Recipes for a Pegan Diet

Recipes That Are Delightful and Simple to Make

Joseph M. Williamson

Contents

Chapter One

Introduction

Dieters who follow the Pegan Diet will benefit from a combination of two very well-known calorie counting methods: the Paleo Diet and the Vegan Diet, amongst others. In order for the Paleo Diet to work, it must be based on our Paleolithic-oeriodoroe:enitors' diettarv oatterns.

Introduction

It is a combination of two very well-known calorie-counting diets - tbc Paleo Diet and tbe Vegan Diet. Tbc Paleo Diet is a low-carb diet that is high in protein and low in carbohydrates. We can trace our ancestors' eating habits back to the Paleolitbic era, and the Paleo Diet includes only those food sources that would have been available prior to the advent of horticulture. Tbe Paleo Diet is based on the nutritional patterns of our Paleolitbic-period ancestors. It includes new eggs, fish, and meat as well as new green vegetables, nuts and seeds, avocado and extra virgin olive oil, spices, and even more spices!

There are no animal products in the Thc Vcgan Diet. This includes egg whites and meat as well as fish and fish products, honey, and dairy products, among other things. Diets such as the Paleolithic diet and the Vegan diet are based on the concept of “whole food sustenance,” which is the concept of discovering new and healthful food sources that have not been significantly altered by man. Dietary requirements from both of these eating regimens are followed by the Pegan Diet, which follows the Paleo Diet principles but prohibits the use of any creature items that would normally be included.

In this book, you will find the information you need as a newcomer to the Pegan diet and practical suggestions for staying active and healthy while following the diet plan. When combined with their nutritional information, Pegan consumes fewer carbohydrates.

Introduction to the Pegan Diet is covered in Chapter One.

Several principles of the paleo diet and vcganism are combined in the Pegan diet, which emphasizes plant-based food. However, even if the two types are sometimes at odds with one another, the overriding feature that peganism receives from both is a stress on authentic, whole food.

varieties.

More vegetables and plants should be consumed, while less processed food should be consumed - these are the opinions expressed at the center.

Those who adhere to the diet consume vegetables as well as organic items such as nuts, seeds, meat, and eggs while abstaining from dairy products, grains, vegetables, sugar, and other processed foods. Sugars, oils, and cereals that have been processed intensively are discouraged - albeit only in little quantities that are satisfactory.

As a temporary feeding pattern, the Pegan diet is not intended to replace a normal food schedule. It anticipates becoming more possible, allowing you to continue to pursue it permanently. Ali things considered

Consumables for the Day of Paganism

It is unmistakably true that the Pegan diet revolves on complete food sources, or food sources that have undergone little processing before they reach your plate.

Limit your intake of fats that have been minimally processed. Solid fats should be obtained from certain sources, such as those listed below.

A,u,,v,Al'lnA l'J;nnC'• f"" lA -" 1n1t::'lt::"1'7AA nliun tnA,..,,l'l'l•lAn n; l nv n, make 1110your plale. A,u,,v,Al'lnA l'J;nnC'•

Remain with the minimally processed falses: Consume solid fa1s from certain sources, such as the ones listed below:

Avocados and olives are two of my favorite foods. It is also possible to use cold-pressed olive and avocado oil.

Omega-3s:

especially from fish with low meromic acid content oralgae

Nuls: All other than peanuls

Seeds: oil extracted from a variety of seeds

It is OK to use unrefined coconut oil.

Pegan diet fats are supplemented by grass-fed, pasture-raised meats and whole eggs, which are sourced locally.

Drink plenty of water and eat plenty of vegetables

For the Pegan diet, vegetables and organic produce are the most important nutrilional categories - they should account for at least 75% of your total calorie consumption.

In order to minimize your glucose reaction, low-glycemic green foods, such as berries and non-slarchy vegetables, should be emphasized.

Small amounts of bland vegetables and sweet organic items may be taken into consideration by those who have already achieved good glucose control prior to commencing the diet.

Protein that has been sourced ethically is preferable.

A adequate amount of protein from animal sources is suggested, despite the fact that the Pegan diet is primarily focused on plant-based food choices.

Keep in mind that whereas vegetables and organic products account for 75 percent of the diet's total calories, just 25 percent of the remaining calories come from animal-based sources of protein. That means you'll consume far less meat than you would on a traditional paleo diet, but you'll consume significantly more than you would on any vegetarian or vegan diet.

Eating frequently farmed meals or eggs loses out to the Pegan diet. All things considered, it places a strong emphasis on grass-fed, field-raised wellsprings of beef, hog, poultry, and whole eggs.

The act also permits the entrance of fish, namely those from Thailand, which will almost always have minimal mercury content and will be as close to wild salmon as is feasible to the target of the law.

The Consumption of Some Whole Grains and Legumes Is Allowable

Granules and vegetables are discouraged from being consumed on the Pegan diet because of their "1 * Y...,...,...,.. salmon

The Consumption of Some Whole Grains and Legumes Is Allowable

However, certain whole grains and vegetables, such as sa ns gluteo whole grains and vegetables, are permitted on the

Pegan diet in limited amounts owing to their capacity to alter glucose.

Grain intake should not exceed a 1/ 2 cup (125 grams) every meal, and vegetable intake should not exceed 1 cup (75 grams) per day.

Some grains and veggies that you may want to try are as follows. Grains: Oats, millet, amaranth, quinoa, and black rice are some of the grains that may be included in a traditional diet. Grains: lentils, chickpeas, black beans and pinto beans are examples of legumes.

However, if you have diabetes or another illness that contributes to the unpleasant glucose crisis, you should restrict your intake of these foods as well.

A list of foods to stay away from

Because it allows for periodicadmission of almost any item, the Pegan diet is more customizable than a paleo or vegetable lover diet.

It is true that certain food kinds and nutritional categories are depleted of energy, as Thai has said. Certain food kinds are recognized to be unhealthy, while others may be thought to be very nutritious.

Dieters following the Pegan diet should avoid the following food sources:

Don't consume any additional sugar, whether refined or unprocessed. You may make use of it on a whim, but not in a conservative fashion.

It is not permitted to consume dairy products such as cheese, cow's milk, or yogurt. Only a little quantity of food items derived from goat and sheep milk are permitted in each instance. Also permitted is the use of a lawn care spread.

Because of their tendency to raise blood glucose levels, legumes are discouraged from being eaten.

It is possible that low-starch veggies such as lentils will qualify.

Gluteo: Ali gluteo-containing grains are discouraged from growing in the environment. Occasionally, a limited amount of whole grain without gluteo may be permitted.

Artificial colorings, flavorings, additives, and other additional compounds are not authorized in the food supply chain.

Highly refined or unusually treated oils, such as canola, soybean, sunflower, and canola oil, are generally discouraged from consumption.

• • • • • • • • • • • • • • • • • • • •

It's U.IUVU...I(U....I(U...I(V...IV....I(U.',,,,,,,,, U U U I IU U U U U U U U U

UUUUUUUUUUUUUUUUUU.::::::::uu.:::::::uuuuuuuuuuuuuuu::::::uuu

Oils that have been refined It is common practice to avoid refined or highly processed oils, such as canola, soybean, sunflower, and coro oil, because of their high flammability.

The majority of these food kinds are prohibited due to their apparent influence on glucose levels or the possibility of causing inflammation in your body, among other reasons.

Glycmic Index (GI) is very high. Fructose and fructose syrups

A higher glycemic index is associated with some natural items. Concentrate on berries and kiwi instead of sugary fruits such as grapes and pineapple, which are rich in vitamin C and antioxidants but low in sugar. Consumption of these more nutritious fruits should still be limited to no more than tban12 cup a day. Eventually, if I want to consume organic products, I'll do it earlier in the day so that I have the opportunity to do so before bedtime. When it comes to glycemic index, apples are at the bottom of the list. Eat them with almond butter to see if it helps to regulate your glucose levels. Also keep in mind that avocados are a naturally occurring product. Aside from the fact that avocado is high in sound fats, it is ranked low on the GJ list. Almost every day, I indulge in a little amount of one of them.

Swcctcncrs

As far as material things go, saccharine and aspartame are a complete disaster. Sugar replacements, including those made from natural sources, We are susceptible to being duped by artificial sweeteners like stevia, which cause insulin and blood sugar levels to rise significantly. Sweetener made from natural sources

Simply put, sugar and high-fructose corn syrup (sometimes known as “stick syrup”) are just different names for the same thing. Agave syrup is not often recommended by dietitians, despite the fact that it is somewhat protected by law, due to its highly refined character. Although coconut and date sugars may be considered equal, there is ongoing debate over whether or not their impact on glucose is precisely the same as or not exactly the same as that of refined pure sweeteners and other sugars. Pegan perfectionists propose reducing sweets in general and choosing sugars that are in their natural condition, such as dates, pure maple syrup, and cancer-fighting crude honey from a small producer, among others (see underneath for more data about craftsman honey). Following a period of abstinence from sugar, you'll notice that a little amount of these sugars goes a long way in terms of calorie consumption.

Making the Best Honey Selection

Analysts discovered that the honey bee population in the United States was beginning to decline around ten years previously. Some suggested that the widespread use of pesticides and even mobile phones (some hypothesized that the proliferation of mobile phones was a factor) were among the reasons why.

Analysts discovered that the honey bee population in the United States had begun to decline around ten years previously. In addition to widespread pesticide use and even the use of mobile phones, other other reasons for wby have been proposed, including (some conjecture that abundance radio waves are making honey beesreturn lost on their way onceagain to the bive). A subsequent increase in the number of beekeepers working to replenish the honey bee population has coincided with an increase in the production of high-quality honey. Tbesecrude boney things are stuffed with celi reinforcements and contamination-fighting antimicrobiasl to make them even more effective. Since these supplements are destroyed by heat, it is critical to use only "cmde"-labeled versions whenever possible. Additionally, I will go to whatever lengths are necessary to avoid include honey in baking preparations. Farmer's markets, boutique retail shops, health food stores, progressive grocery stores, and even a neighbor's garden are all good places to look for artisanal honey.

Beverages that are Pegan Friendly

Separated water, the good old days

A squeeze of lemon or lime in filtered water

For the time being, homemade nut milks may be created by dousing nuts in a bowl with a little sifting water and vanilla extract (optional), then mixing it all together.

Use non-BPA jars or recyclable containers for your coconut milk!

Drink warm water mixed with lemon or a little amount of apple cider vinegar.

With or without sugar or sugar substitutes, dark or with a little amount of medium-chain fatty acids (MCFA)•substance oil or unsweetened coffee

Chapter Two

the milk made from nuts

Green, rooibos, black, or homegrown teas, without sugar or milk

Use coconut water sparingly.

Electrolyte pills added to water

The use of clear fluids in cocktails is recommended since studies have shown that they contain less sugar overall and may have a less detrimental effect on glucose levels than bourbon, Scotch, and other earthy-colored liquors. Specific to Tequila, it was shown to have the least impact on glucose levels in the blood. In addition, it has less calories than vodka, which is often made from grains and is more expensive. You could want to skip the too sweet margarita mix and instead go for completing your tequila with seltzer water and a squeeze of lime, or a little obfuscating with mint leaves.

Pegan Diet Has Many Health Advantages

There are several benefits to following the Pegan diet, with weight loss being the most significant of these perks. But there are other,s as well, and when these things,vork ali together, not only does it assist in dropping the number on the scale, but it also aids in clearer thinking and helps lead to an.

There are several benefits to following the Pegan diet, with the primary one being weight loss. The fact is that there are otbers as well, and when these tbings work together, not only does tbat assist to lower the tbc scale, but it also helps in clearer tbinking and belps lead to an overall happier environment! ife.

1. Makes it possible to assist without effort Tbat last word is really crucial in terms of weight loss. Sugar and carbohydrates, according to scientific evidence, are swiftly converted to fat when not consumed. On the other hand, since they are not processed by the liver, saturated fats, which are a staple of the Pegan diet, are not stored as fat. Even more so, over a long period of time, the body prefers to use fat as an energy source rather than carbs or basic sugars. If you're not running big distances or working out for hours every day, you're not going to be able to eat the calories that have been stored in your body from sugar and unhealthy carbohydrates. Even more concerning is the fact that many people work in the same place on a consistent basis. However, eating the Pegan method is not just beneficial in terms of calorie intake and expenditure. It's more about how many calories you consume

and when you consume them, specifically. In other words, it's focusing on the substance of our food selections rather than the quantity of our food choices. There will be no calorie counting! You heard it correctly. It also seems to be functional. I was able to lose the final few of pounds I had been carrying about for a long time during the beginning of the process of putting this book together, when I paid more attention to my own advice. As has also been the case with Furtbennorethey, Retains Control Over Cravings: Ever had an uncontrollable yearning for Ben & Jerry's ice cream, pizza at any time of day, bagels or bready sandwiches? Or for chocolate in any form (or even just a few squares)? Prior to adopting a Paleo, then a Pegan, diet, they were some of my most intense desires. Why these high-protein, low-carb, low-orno-sugar diets that consume fewer calories are effective has a scientific basis. Starches and any sort of sugar, even if it is a synthetic sugar, can cause insulin levels to jump significantly. Assuming you consume carbohydrates or sugars throughout the most of the day, regardless of whether it is deemed solid, such as a squeezed orange, whole wheat bread, or gluteo pasta, insulin levels will remain elevated throughout the day, even into the evening. This may result in insulin blockage in the case of prediabetes and type 2 diabetes. It should go without saying that veggies contain carbohydrates. However, because of their high fiber content, they do not have the same effect on glucose levels. In addition to this, beans and grains are very rich in fiber, but they also include a lot of starchy carbohydrates that are difficult to burn, which is why the Pegan diet defines ideal options and promotes moderation in this d ll t:lUY UUViuUU:>, Vt: t:ldUI dH t:dl UUU:>, d:> Dt! lUd l d::> Wt:11, Dt! lUd l d::> Because of their high fiber content, they do not have the same effect on blood glucose levels. According to the Pegan diet, beans and grains are likewise high in fiber, but they also include a significant amount of starchy carbohydrates that are difficult to digest, which is why the diet recommends making optimum selections and encouraging moderation in this category. In addition to having compulsion-like characteristics, carb consumption causes urges for ever more carbohydrates (don't blame yourself for not having self-control!). Excess insulin may result in a greasy liver, similar to the effects of excessive alcohol use. The yikes are multiplied double. It helps you lose belly fat while keeping your lean muscle. Now for the kicker: as we already know, ingesting too many handled food sources and inadequate whole, fresh food sources might result in persistent aggravation in the body's organs. Continuous irritation not only sets the stage for the development of potentially dangerous diseases, but it also causes cortisol levels to rise, which may put you in a state of constant stress and discomfort. Sadly, the regrettable reaction to such chemical discomfort is put away instinctivefat, the dreadful fat that collects around key organs and causes waistlines to get larger. By focusing on a diverse array of whole-food kinds in their most natural form while also avoiding dairy, you may prevent these hormonal shifts that cause gut fat to accumulate. In addition, you have it-by losing belly fat, you will also lose weight overall. Although wbile practice is not the primary focus of this book, adding even a little amount of solidarity preparation to your standard will aid in assisting the powers of the Pegan way of life. Increased muscular definition will be seen. Tummy ache due to cootrasted food.

Consuming calories more efficiently throughout the day is beneficial for fat, fit mass. After reaching your weight loss target, it is critical to maintain your newfound stability. Appetite is controlled by: By interfering with leptin in the brain, too much insulin may also cause troubles with cravings and contro). Irrespective of whether or not your body gets the energy it need, you'll assume you're starving. In addition, by focusing on selecting high-quality, whole food sources the most of the time rather than counting calories, you'll be able to better gauge how much food you're really craving when you sit down to dinner or grab a quick snack on the go. Your body will learn what it genuinely feels like to be truly famished, and you will be able to provide it with just what it requires.. You will also get more familiar with what it feels like to be completely satisfied, despite the fact that the Pegan diet is based on eating until you're just about full, rather than sated. In addition, isn't it true that it's a little tough to stufi oneself with broccoli? When your ability to view the big picture improves, you will most likely eat less as a general rule, which, as you may have guessed, results in greater weight reduction!

Mentality should be elevated. Boosts Clarity and Energizes You: It's like getting a shock.

Isn't it true that you have to load yourself with broccoli since it's tough to do it in 10 minutes? As your ability to perceive a sense of tolalily develops, you will most likely eal lessasa generai rule, which, as you have already seen, results with greater weight loss. Increase Mentality Elevates the senses and brings clarity Energy: Astonishingly powerful is the surge of energy that comes from kicking handledcarbs and sugars to the curb! Anyway, it was a long way away from where I was standing. There are a total of ten factors that contribute to it: Incorporating more sugar into your diet can help you avoid enatic, emotional and addiction-like behaviors as well as cravings for unhealthy foods. Additionally, by increasing our intake of foods high in omega-3 fatty acids, such as avocadoes, walnuts, grass-fed hamburger and spread, and low-mercury fish, we are sending more energy to and taking better care of our mind. Glucose has been known to increase the firing rate of neurons for a long time. Sound fats are not only very beneficial to heart health, but they are also beneficial to the intellect and nerve health, according to recent research. Beyond the psychological clarity you will get from eating vegetables and other foods in their natural condition, eating vegetables and other foods in their natural state will provide you with more energy than you could have anticipated to go through your day. vili Cholesterol: It is possible that your total cholesterol level may rise as a result of eating the Pegan method for an extended period of time, as was the case for me. That is most likely due to an increase in good cholesterol levels (HDLs), independent of whether or not the bad cholesterol levels (LDLs) stay the same or, even better, decline in the meanwhile. At this time, neither fai nor eggs have been submerged in water.

They were always portrayed as miscreants, no matter what. But processed foods and oils, along with sugar and processed carbohydrates, have all been linked to high blood pressure and high cholesterol levels, which may lead to coronary artery disease. You may eat that solid fat as much as you like; just be sure to choose feed proteins and nontoxic fish to ensure you're receiving omega-3 unsaturated fats rather than the potentially harmful omega-6 unsaturated fats found in meat from corn-fed animals and processed meals.

The Pegan Pantry offers a variety of meats and poultry, including grass-fed beef.

A bison that has been fed just grass.

Grass-fed butter is the best!

No antibiotics are used in the production of chickens, whether they are fed or raised naturally.

Farm-raised or organic game, eggs, and poultry elkor venison is a kind of venison that comes from the Elkor region of Africa.

The letters “u vvu, b,“UVV "″-” Butter and gras.5-fed

Antibiotic-free chicken, whether fed or natural

Either organic or fed game such as elk or venison is used.

grass-fed lamb is the best kind of lamb.

Pork that has been fed or that has been raised without using a box

Turkey, pasturecl, and pasturecl.

The word “afood” is an abbreviation for “Sc afood.”

Canned or fresh Arctic Singe, wild Cod Clams, canned or fresh Crab, canned or fresh Flounder Herring, wild-caught Lobster Mackerel, Atlantic or Pacific Mussels

Oysters

Alaskan salmon (wild or farmed), tinned salmon, or both.

Saigon-style sardines, either freshly caught or canned

Scallops

Shrimp\sSnapper

Tilapia\sTrout

fresh or canned tuna, tuna line-got, tuna line-got

Fruit to be grown: red apples

Artichoke hearts in a water-based dressing.

Avocados

Prewashed, sacked, or fresh baby spinach are all good options for you.

the freshest basil

Beets

Green, red, yellow, or orange bell peppers are included in this dish as well.

Berries (blueberries, strawberries, raspberries, or blackberries) (fresh or frozen, in season or frozen)

Napa cabbage (bokchoy) and redor napa (napa cabbage).

CARROTS FOR THIRTY-ONE PERCENT OF THE WORLD'S CARROTS FOR THIRTY-ONE PERCENT OF THE WORLD'S CARROTS FOR THIRTY-ONE PERCENT OF THE WORLD "and/or 01acKoemesJ or 01acKoemesJ

Cabbage, either red or napa, bokchoy (bokchoy).

Carrots

Chardonnay, Swiss chard, or rainbow chard are all excellent choices.

Fresh cilantro, fresh basil, fresh dill, fresh parsley, fresh parsley, fresh parsley

Cucumber\sEggplant

Garlic

Cinger

Beans from Greco

Kale\sLemons

You may choose from lettuce varieties such as Boston, Bibb, red leaf, and romaine.

Limes

Mushrooms

Olives

Red onions or yellow onions are used for slicing.

Using fresh oregano

Lettuce, leaflettuce, leaflettuce

Peppers, jalapenos, and oregano are among the ingredients.

Chapter Three

The scent of rosemary is intoxicating.

Various squashes, include butternut and spaghetti, as well as oakseed, yellow, and summer squashes

Scallions

Shallots

Cauliflower is a kind of root vegetable that is native to the United States.

Tomatoes,fresh\sTomatillos

Zucchini

Pcs. Spicing up the picture

The bay leaves are a kind of plant that is native to the Mediterranean region.

peppercorns (also known as black pepper)

Cayenne pepper is a hot pepper that is used to spice up food.

Cayenne pepper et c.

Cinnamon, cumin powder, and curry powder are all spices.

Cayenne pepper et c.

Grounded Cinnamon and Curry Powder are some of the most popular spices.

Turmeric root powder (sometimes known as garlic powder) is a spice that may be used to flavor foods.

nutmeg, onion powder (whole), and cayenne

The dried herb oregano (also known as oregano).

Paprika, scorching hot, sweet, or smoked

flakes of red pepper

Salt is a mineral compound found in nature (oceao salt and pink salt arethe most regular sor ts and containthe most su pplemetns; litsalt is additionallygood)

Thyme leaves that have been dry

Spices and condiments for the turmeric kitchen

Avocado oil is a kind of oil that comes from avocados.

Unsalted cacao powder, raw coconut drops, and unsweetened cocoout oil are all ingredients in this recipe.

Medicinal dates, Medjool dates, Medjool dates, Medjool dates, Dates

Honey, unprocessed, sourced from reliable sources (seeChoosing the Right Honey)

No additives, just hot sauce

No additives, just pure maple syrup.

Miso Mustard, Dijon Nori sheets, Miso Mustard, Dijon Nori sheets, Miso Mustard

Yeast that is good for you

No sugar or chemicals in this extra-virgin olive oil salsa made using cold-pressed olive oil.

The oil derived from sesame is used in a variety of applications.

lorcoconut aminos, soysauce, sansgluteo, tamar, and tamari

Sriracha

tempeh tofu, sprouting tomatoes with no extra sugar or salt, smashed, sliced, orentire, packaged in a box

Vanilla, exceptionally pure and unadulterated, with no alcoholic content.

A variety of vinegars, balsamic vinegars, red fennel juice, sherry vinegars, rice vinegars and coconut vinegars

tomatoes, no sugar or basil added, smashed, cleaved, or whole tomatoes, packaged in a box of

Authentic vanilla extract, pure and free of alcohol.

Vinegars, balsamic vinegar, red wine, juice, sherry, rice, and cocoout are all examples of condiments that are used.

Paste made from wasabi (also known as wasabi sauce)

Foods that are suitable for vegetarians and vegans

30 Second Egg, also known as hard-bubbledegg, is an egg that has been hard-bubbled for at least 30 seconds.

There is an abundance of crude outs in Haodfui.

Sprinkled with almond or cashew butter and topped with celery leaves

No matter what warm sauce you use, onelittle or one-halfenormotL avocado will do.

With or without butter, appies orkalecbips

PeganBreakfast Recipes (Chapter Two):

Ketogenic With avocado and baked eggs, this dish is a must-try.

2 people can eat this dish.

20 minutes are required for preparation. Ingredients

Use a nonstick spray to keep things from sticking together.

Spiralized zucchini noodles (three zucchinis)

extra-virgin olive oil (about 2 teaspoons).

Sea salt with freshly ground black pepper (kosher salt and freshly ground black pepper)

4 colossal ovaries

Garnish with red pepper flakes if desired

Garnish with fresh basi (basil).

a couple of avocados, peeled and split with a few slices

Directions

Preheat the broiler to 350 degrees Fahrenheit. 2.

Nonstick spray should be used sparingly on a baking pan.

In a large mixing basin, toss the zucchini noodles with the olive oil to combine. Sea salt and freshly ground pepper are used for seasoning. Divide the dough into four equal pieces and place each on a baking sheet, forming a nest with each.

To make each nest, gently crack one egg into the foca! point at the top.

Bake for 9 to 11 minutes, or until the eggs are firm. Season with salt and pepper, then garnish with red-pepper chips and a basi!

Ideally, the avocado slices should be served near by as well.

Tnformation in the Nutritional Sciences: 6 calories from fat.i i. Carhs 2 71 calories from carbohydrate

. . . .
. . . .
. . . . —- —-
—- —- —- —- —- —- —- —- —- —- —- —- —- —- —- —- —- —-
—- —- —- —- —- —- —- —- —- —- —- —- —- —- —- —- —- —-
—- Season with salt and pepper, and garnish with red-pepper cbips and basil, if desired.

The avocado slices should be served right next to the dish. 6.

Nutritional Information (Information on Nutrition): A total of 633 calories, 53 grams of fat, 27 grams of carbohydrates, and 20 grams of protein

Vegetable Frittata

The number of services is six.

Ingredients Preparation time: one hour

1 pepperoncini, diced 1 zucchini, diced 2 garlic cloves, minced 1 tablespoon olive oil or 1/4 cup water (for watersauté) 1 tablespoon ehime peppe or 1/4 cup water (for watersauté)

diced 2 medium-sized potatoes (despite eve1ything tbeskin)

1 small onion, a diced small bunch of grape tomatoes, a split or quartered toucb of red pepper piece, optional minerai salt and newbroke pepper, and tot taste

In the case of a blender or food processor,

mustard (any variety) or 1/2 teaspoon mustard powder (optional)

dried tarragon, thyme, or basil (1 1/2 teaspoons) (ora combo)

garlic powder (1/2 teaspoon)

1-1/2 teaspoons sodium chloride

turmeric (one-fourth teaspoon)

white or dark pepper, to taste (optional).

Directions

Cook at 375 degrees Fahrenheit on an induction stovetop.

In a large skillet, heat the oil over medium heat until shimmering. Add the potatoes and cook for 5 minutes more.

Cook until the chile pepper, zucchini, and garlic are tender, but not mushy, for about 15 minutes. Cook for a few minutes longer after adding the tomatoes and optional red pepper chip. Taste and season with salt and pepper to your preference. In a food processor, combine all of the leftover ingredients and pulse until completely smooth. Check the seasoning with a taste test before serving. Combine the tofu mixture with the vegetables that have been cooking in the dish. Pour the mixture into a round pie/quiche dish

or springform pan that has been lightly lubricated with melted butter. leve) the uppermost leve) with the rear of one one one one one one one one one one one one one "The year 2011 was one of transition. Combine the tofu mixture with the vegetables that have been cooked in the dish and mix thoroughly. To serve, spoon the mixture into a round pie/quiche dish or springform container that has been delicately lubricated. Leve! the topleve! with the back of an aspatula or a spoon and make sure the ali edges are filled with liquid. Preheat the oven to 350°F and bake for 35-45 minutes, or until the frittata is firm when touched with a finger. Wrapping the top with aluminum foil or a small piece of silpat will help prevent it from browning too much. After removing the pan from the heat, let it cool for at least 10 minutes.
For those using a pie or quiche dish, loosen the edges of the frittata and carefully flip it over so that the frittata falls onto the piate and is ready to be served (this step is not required).

If you add chopped avocado and a dash of hot sauce, this frittata is out of this world.

Informaiton nutritionnelle 226, 9.5 grams of fat, 22.3, grams of carbohydrate, and 16.1 grams of protein

Avocado Baked Eggs are a delicious way to start your morning.

The number of services is two, and the preparation time is twenty minutcs. Ingredicnts split and pit 2 medium or eoormous avocados, depending on size

4 colossal ovaries

peppercorns that have been freshly ground

Preheat the broiler to 425 degrees Fahrenheit in step one.

Using the avocado parts as scooping tools, scoop out a portion of the mash, leaving enough room for an egg and reserving the remaining mash for Easy Guacamole (see the formula Ceviche Fish Tacos with Easy Guacamole).

Aluminum foil should be used to line a baking dish 8 by 8 inches. Place the avocado pieces in the skillet so that they fit snugly in a single layer, then wrap aluminum foil around the outside of the avocados to prevent them from tipping over during preparation. Season with pepper after cracking 1 egg into each avocado half. Unti, the heat has been revealed. 12 to 15 minutes later, the egg whites will be set and the egg yolks will be cooked to your liking.

Allow for 5 minutes of resting time after removing from the broiler.

NutritionalInformation: 433 calories, 34 grams of fat, 16 grams of carbohydrates, and 16 grams of protein.

serving.

The following is the nutritional data: T6 grams of protein and 430 calories. Fats: 34 grams. Carbohydrates: 6 grams.

Bacon-Wrapped Brussels Sprouts with Garlic Balsamic Glaze 6.

5 services; preparation time: 35 minutes Ingredients

sugar free bacon for the whole family (4-6 cuts nitrate free)

30 pepperoncini di Saliando

2 pounds (split) brussel sprouts (orquartered for biggerones)

1 pound minced garlic, 4 garlic cloves

Balsamic vinegar (about 2 tablespoons)

Directions

Prepare your stove by preheating it to 425 degrees.

A large baking sheet with a single layer of brussels sprouts is ideal for this.

Cut the bacon into pieces, and then sprinkle the ali over the Brussels sprouts once the bacon has been chopped.

Preheat the broiler to high heat for 15 minutes before turning the broiler down to low heat and baking for another 15 minutes.

Return to a single layer and continue to cook for another 5-10 minutes, or until the bacon is crisped up.

Garlic should be sprinkled on after the vinegar has been drizzled.

Stir occasionally for another 5-7 minutes, or until the chicken is seared and crispy.

Always good as an aperitif dish! Enjoy!

The following is the nutritional data: 82 calories, 6 grams of fat, 2 grams of carbohydrate, and 2 grams of protin

Muffins made with vegetables and eggs

Serves:2

30 minutes are required for preparation. Ingredients For lubrication (optional), extra-virgin olive oil, coconut oil, orexplained s pread are recommended. It's a lot of numbers, but it's a lot of fun. Extra-virgin olive oil, coconut oil, or explainedspread can be used to lubricate joints and muscles (optional)

Large eggs (twelve in number).

sea salt or Himalayan salt (about 2 teaspoons)

freshly ground black pepper (about 2 teaspoons)

1 medium-sized red ehime pepper, cultivated and finely chopped

Cultivated and diced: 1 medium orange, yellow, or green ringer pepper, depending on the variety.

chopped finely 1 cup stuffing for children's spinach

Scallions that have been delicately cut (112)

1. 1 cultivated and minced jalapeiio pepper (small jalapeio) (optional)

Dircctions

350 degrees Fahrenheit should be set for the broiler. Use paper biscuit liners or oil a 12-hole biscuit tin with 12 openings. Pour all of the ingredients into a large mixing bowl and whisk until well combined (about 3 minutes). Using a mixer or a fork, combine the peppers, spinach, scallions, and jalapeio.

Make an even layer of egg mixture in the biscuit pan that has been previously set up.

Bake for about 20 minutes, or until a toothpick or paring biade confesses ali when inserted. 10 minutes before serving, remove the biscuits from the skillet and set aside to cool.

The following is the nutritional data: 82% of calories come from fat (6g), and only 2% of calories come from carbohydrates.

egg whites (vegetarian) 2 g protein

Chapter Four

Lemon Hollandaise Sauce on a Benedict Casserole

Approximately 18 minutes to prepare for 2 people. Hollandia Sauce is made up of several ingredients.

the yolks of three large eggs (save whites for other use)

Extra-virgin olive oil, ghee, or butter (as directed) 12 cup

1 tablespoon freshly squeezed lemon juice (from approximately 12 lemons)

a pinch of salt and a pinch of cayenne pepper

2 teaspoons apple cider vinegar or white vinegar for each egg.

Pinch-button cayenue peppers

2 teaspoonsappie juicevinegaror wbite vinegar for each egg

4 colossal ovaries

1-inch-thick beefsteak or treasuretornato, closed-eliminated, cut into four thick slices

lices

Spinach, 1 cup (cbild),

peppercorns that have been freshly harvested

Directions

Pour boiling water into a pot and fill it up to about 4 inches up the sides of the pot to make the hollandaise sauce. Discard the hot water, which amounts to 2 tablespoons. Egg yolks should be whisked in a medium metal mixing bowl. In a large mixing bowl, whisk together the olive oil, high-temperature water, lemon juice, salt, and cayenne. In a bowl of bubbling water, float the bowl on the surface. Stir constantly until the sauce is thickened, 1 to 2 minutes, while keeping the bowl away from the boiling water to prevent the eggs from souring on the bottom of the bowl. Discard the bowl of hollandaise sauce from the pot of boiling water and set it to one side on another piece of stovetop utensil The botness of the eggs should be reduced by adding them to a pot of boiling water and simmering for a while. Organize a paper-towel station.

dish that has been lined Carefully crack the eggs into a small bowl one at a time, then use the bowl to gently slide two of the eggs into the water. 2 minutes of simmering time is recommended for this recipe. Transfer the eggs to a plate lined with paper towels, using an opened spoon to help you along. Go back and look at what happened with the extra two eggs. Using two plates, divide the tornato slices and serve immediately. Season the top of each tornato with a few spinach leaves, 1 poached egg, and 2 heaping tablespoons of warm hollandaise sauce. Serve immediately after seasoning with black pepper.

The following is the nutritional data: There are 423 calories, 39 grams of fat, 6 grams of carbs, and 16 grams of protein in this recipe.

Smoothie made with strawberries and coconut that is Paleo-friendly.

2 people can eat this dish.

Minutes required for preparation: 5 2 cups frozen strawberries are needed for this dish.

Timing for the pre-parati on: 5 minutes 2 cups frozen s trawberreis are used in this recipe.

vanilla extract (about 1 teaspoon)

Coconut milk (about 1 cup)

banana (frozen) sliced 1 banana

Protein powder made from gelatin and collagen.

Directions

1.

In a large high-speed blender, combine the ali fixings and blend until smooth.

The term “nutrition” refers to the act of adding nutrients to food to make it more nutritious. 376 calories, 24 grams of fat, 27 grams of carbohydrates, and one gram of protein

Pumpkin Pancakes with a Spiced Flour Topping

10 minutes for preparation. Scrves: 5 minutes total preparation time: 10 minutes total. Cups of pumpkin puree (in grated form) (11/3 cup)

Whistled together are six enormous eggs.

To 1 tablespoon coconut flour, add 2 tablespoons pure maple syrup (1/ 2 cup) and mix thoroughly.

ground cinnamon (about 1 teaspoon)

Nutmeg (ground) to 1/4 teaspoon

salt (about a pinch)

chopped pecans (about 1/2 cup) (optional)

Directions

Over medium heat, heat a large nonstick skillet to 350°F or higher. Combine the pumpkin, eggs, maple syrup, and vanilla extract in a food processor and process until well combined and smooth. At that point, add the coconut flour along with the spices (cinnamon, nutmeg, salt) and blend until smooth. Using approximately 3 tablespoons for each pancake, spoon the player into the hot skillet. Add a couple of slashed pecans to the wet bitter and cook for 1 to 2 minutes, or until the underside is lightly browned. Cook the flapjacks for a few more minutes on the other side, until they are lightly sautéed. Reheat the hotcakes on a plate to keep them warm while you prepare the remaining batter.

Continue to make flapjacks and cook until unti returns!

Underside has been sautéed.

5. Transfer the hotcakes to a plate to keep them warm while you re-batter them with the remainder of the batter.

Informaiton nutritionnelle 250 calories, 15 grams of fat, 19 grams of carbohydrate, and 13 grams of protein per serving.

6.

Healthy Nutty Granola Made Without Using Grains

2 people can eat this dish.

Approximately 32 minutes are required for preparation.

Ingredients

crude pecans or pecans slashed in 1112 cups

2 cups chopped raw almonds 112 cups seeds, toasted or simmered unsalted sunflower, sesame, or pumpkin 1 cup chopped raw almonds

13/14 cup coconut flakes, unsweetened

I used 12 cup coconut oil or unsalted gra&'J to take care of the s pread, and it worked perfectly.

1 tablespoon of molasses

1 teaspoon pure vanilla extract (no booze or alcohol added).

or to your liking 1 teaspoon ground cinnamon

Sea salt (or Himalayan salt) to taste (about 1/4 teaspoon).

Directions

1. Preheat the oven to 300 degrees Fahrenheit (150 degrees Celsius).

Using parchment paper or aluminum foil, line the rim of a baking sheet.

10 large mixing basin, mix together the pecans, almonds, seeds and coconul pieces. In a separate basin, combine the oil, mapie symp, vanilla, cinnamon, and salt and whisk until well combined. Add 1hrov1fog to lhe nul blend and mix well. Heat till golden brown, about 25 minutes, spreading the mixture evenly on a baking sheet that has been pre-arranged. Stir once halfway through. Completely and utterly refreshing.

The following is the nutritional data: 248, 25 grams of fat, 6 grams of carbohydrates, and 4 grams of protein

Asparagus and Tomatoes in a One-Pan Egg Salad

Serves:2

Approximately 32 minutes are required for preparation.

To make 2 servings of tomatoes, cut them in half and place them on a baking sheet in the middle of the kitchen.

Approximately 32 minutes are required for preparation.

Ingredients

egg whites (four)

olive oil (around 2 tbsp.

Asparagus, two pounds

tomatoe (about 16 ounces) 1

2-tablespoons new tbyme (cleaved)

to taste with salt and pepper

Directions

To begin, preheat the broiler to 400 degrees Fahrenheit. Spray a baking sheet with non-stick cooking spray before starting the baking process. Prepare the baking sheet by arranging the asparagus and cherry tomatoes in a uniform layer. Season with the thyme, sali, and pepper to taste and drizzle the olive oil over the veggies. Cook on the stove for a long time. Asparagus is practically delicate, and the tomatoes have been increased in cooking time (about 10 to 12 minutes). Season the eggs with salt and pepper and place them on top of the asparagus.

Go back to your broiler and finish off your unti. tbeegg wbites haven't been determined yet.

7 to 8 minutes longer until the yolks are still jiggly.

Assemble four individual dishes by dividing the asparagus, tomatoes, and eggs amongst them.

The following is the nutritional data:

It has 158 calories and 13 grams of fat. It has 0 grams of carbohydrates and 8 grams of protein.

Served with Blueberry Syrup, Mini Pegan Pancakes.

Pancakes are around 12 in number. 20 minutes are required for preparation. Ingredients

Banana that is really ripe

large eggs (there are 2 of them)

One-fourth cup liquor freevanilla flavoring

Cinnamon powder (about 1 teaspoon)

Squeeze in a pinch of ocean or Himalayan salt.

- s - s - s - s - s - s - s

1, 2, 3, 4, 5, 6, 7, 8, 9, 10, 11, 12, 13, 14, 15, 16, 17, 18, 19, 20, 21, 22, 23, 24, 25, 26, 27, 28, 29, 30, 31, 32

large eggs (there are 2 of them)

Vanilla extract made without the use of alcoholic beverages

cinnamon powder (about 1 teaspoon)

The Himalayan salt (also known as ocean salt or Himalayan salt)

split into 14 cup coconut oil or explained margarin

2-cups of blueberries, either fresh or frozen

Directions

1-Pulse the banana until it is completely mellowed in a medium-sized mixing basin.

Toss in the eggs and pound until the mixture is smooth and the overwhelming majority of the pieces have been combined, about 3 minutes. Combine the vanilla, cinnamon, and salt in a separate bowl until well combined.

2. In a large skillet or level cast iron container, heat one tablespoon of the coconut oil over medium heat until it is hot. In a 3-inch mold, pour in 2–3 tablespoons of the bitter to form the mold. Continue to cook until the hotcakes are set and brilliant brown, 2 to 4 minutes ali out per side, flipping

once during the cooking process. Transfer to a cooling plate. Continue to cook until the bitterness has been completely eliminated, adding 1 tablespoon coconut oil in the middle of each batch.. The blueberries and 1 tablespoon coconut oil should be placed in a separate, small pot. Cook, stirring constantly with a wooden spoon, over medium heat for 3 to 5 minutes, or until juices have reduced to a syrup-like consistency. Remove from the heat and place somewhere cool to rest.

Flapjacks should be served with a side of blueberry syrup.

InformatioN on Nutrients: A 224-calorie meal contains 17 grams of fat, 18 grams of carbohydrates, and

Carrot Cinnamon Muffi ns (16.11g protein)

Prepared in 20 minutes, this dish will serve 12. Ingredients

Almond flour (about 2 cups)

ground cinnamon (about 1 teaspoon)

Baking soda, 1 teaspoon

ground ginger (1/2 teaspoon)

salt (one-quarter teaspoon)

I had three enormous eggs, which were all wbisked perfectly.

apple sauce (without sugar, 12 cup)

Mapiesyrup, unadulterated, 1/2 cup

fresh grated carrots (one cup)

Directions

l/:,

Welp, it's the end of the world, and the end of the world is a çupULL WTTTLLUT!

Aaaaaaaaaaaaaaaaa

the letter "U" stands for "United States of America."

1/2 cup pure maple syrup (unadulterated).

3 carrots, peeled and grated

Dircctions

1.

Prepare a biscuit dish with paper liners and preheat the broiler to 350°F.

Using a large mixing bowl, combine all of the dry ingredients.

Eggs, fruit purée, and maple syrup are whisked together in a separate bowl. The carrot should be combined with the liquid ingredients before being combined with the dry ingredients at the halfway point. s Bitter should be placed in the biscuit skillet, filling each cup about two-thirds of the way. Hcat for the next 18 to 20 minutes! It is possible to remove a biade that has been inserted in the centre.

The following is the nutritional data: 90 calories, 4 grams of fat, 12 grams of carbohydrate, and 1 gram of protein per serving 3g

Sweet Potatoes with a Sautéd Garlic Sauce Hash

Scrves:4

20 minutes are required for preparation. Ingredients

Coconutoil, 2 tablespoons

two baby acorn squashes, peeled and sliced

Water in the amount of 3 teaspoons

little yellow onion, chopped little cauliflower, lower florets 1 cup cleaved cauliflower

mushroom chunks (about 1 cup)

to taste with salt and pepper

Directions

1. In a large pan, heat the coconut oil over medium heat until shimmering. Toss in the yams, making sure to coat them completely with the yam mixture "Add the oil first, then the water after that. Allow for 8 to 10 minutes of simmering time, or until the yams are soft and tender.

After you've added the onion, broccolini and mushrooms, give it another stir. Cook another 4 to 6 minutes, or until the onion is transparent, depending on your preference.

Season with salt and pepper to taste, and then serve immediately after preparing it.

The following is the nutritional data: 3g of protein per serving. 210 calories. 7g of fat. 35g of carbs.

In this dish, eggs are served with asparagus and tomato sauce on the side.

The following is the nutritional data: 210 calories, 7 grams of fat, 35 grams of carbohydrate, and 3 grams of protein

In this dish, eggs are served with asparagus and tomato sauce on the side.

Prepared in 32 minutes, this dish serves 2. Ingredients

egg whites (four)

olive oil (around 2 tbsp.

2 teaspoons fresh thyme, cut into small pieces

Asparagus, 2 pound

the weight of one to sixteen ounces. cherry tomatoes are a kind of tomato that is small and round in shape, with a thin skin.

to taste with salt and pepper

Directions

Prepare the stove by preheating it to 400° F.

Prepare a baking sheet by spraying it with nonstick cooking spray and allowing it to sit for 15 minutes.

Using a baking sheet, evenly distribute the asparagus and cherry tomatoes in a single layer.

Season the veggies with the thyme and salt and pepper to taste after drizzling the olive oil on top of them.

Put the broiler on high for a few minutes.

It takes 10 to 12 minutes to cook the asparagus until it is nearly delicate and the tomatoes are severely wrinkled

Season the eggs with salt and pepper and place them on top of the asparagus.

Go back to your broiler and finish off your unti. 7 to 8 minutes longer, or until the egg whites are set but the yolks are still jiggly Using four dishes, divide the asparagus, tomatoes, and eggs among them and serve immediately.

The following is the nutritional data: calories: 158, fats: ug, carbohydrates: 13g, protein: ug.

Chapter Five

Meat and Chicken Recipes

Peppers with Picadillo Stuffing

There are two types of services available.

35 minutes are required for preparation. Ingredients

2 chile peppers (red, yellow, orange, or green)

35 minutes are required for preparation. Ingrcdicnts

A mixture of 2 cbime peppers (red, yellow, orange, or green)

extra virgin olive oil (three teaspoons, divided)

1-pound of cbicken or ground grass-took care of the meat.

Ground cumin (1 tablespoon)

Stewpowder, 1 tablespoon

ground cinnamon (11 1/2 teaspoons)

14 teaspoon salt 14 teaspoon freshly grated black pepper 14 teaspoon freshly grated white pepper

Pepper, a pinch of cayenne (optional)

3 tablespoons finely sliced yellow or sweet onion

miuced 2 cloves of garlic

2 pounds ripe plum tomatoes, chopped with liquids saved

1 cup pitted or pimento-stuffed green olives, quartered 12 cups fresh cilantro, shaved finely

Directions

Preheat the broiler to 400 degrees Fahrenheit. 1.

Remove the seeds from the peppers and cut them into equal-sized pieces, keeping the stem intact. Cover with 1 tablespoon olive oil and arrange on a baking sheet coated with aluminum foil, cut-side up. Toss the meat in a medium-sized mixing basin with the cumin, stew powder, cinnamon, salt, dark pepper, and cayenne pepper until well combined (if using). Using a large skillet, heat 1 tablespoon of the oil on a medium heat setting. Cook for about 2 minutes, or until the meat is delicately sautéed but not fully done. Using an opened spoon, transfer to a bowl.

Heat the remaining 1 tablespoon of oil in a similar skillet. Cook for about 2 minutes, stirring occasionally, until the onion is delicate and clear. Cook for about 30 seconds, or until the garlic is aromatic.

Combine the tomatoes and their juices, the olives, and the cilantro in a large mixing bowl until well combined.

Fill the ringer pepper halves halfway with the mixture.

Allow 10 to 15 minutes for the peppers to become tender and any excess tornato liquids to be completely gone. Remove from the heat, let it cool a little, and then plate up for serving.

The following is the nutritional data: 768 calories, 49 grams of fat, 29 grams of carbohydrate, and 51 grams of protein

Chicken Fennel Bake Serves:2..............".... -...........................".

—-·..,...-;,,

Chicken Fennel Bake with 51 grams of protein per serving

35 minutes are required for preparation. Ingredie nts are substances that are used to make things.

the juice of five lemons.

extra-virgin olive oil (14 cups)

potatoes (child) weighing 1 pound 1 pound 1 pound

2-fennel-bulb mixture with trimmed Kosber sali and freshly ground dark pepper

Carrots (about 1 cup)

Cbickenthighs (six thighs):

Dircctions

Preheat the broiler to 375 degrees Fahrenheit before you start cooking. Remove the foil from the baking sheet. Thinly slice the beef with a sharp knife to create tbc feancl iato thick slices It's time to focus on Sbiaglc! Preheat the oven to 350°F. Sprinkle salt and pepper over the baked beans. Set aside 2 lemoas with their zests and set them aside. At that time, squeeze the lemoas into a medium-sized mixing bowl and set them aside. In a separate bowl, whisk together the olive oil, lemon juice, and salt & pepper.

Cut the remaining three lemons in halves and place them in the bowl with the rest of the lemons.

The potatoes and carrots are the main ingredients.

Toss your coat in the laundry basket.

Vegetables and lemon segments should be spread around the outside of the baking sheet. Place the chicken thighs in a large mixing basin with the lemon zest and juice, as well as more salt and pepper to taste. Toss your coat in the laundry basket. Make a bed of the fennel and place the chicken on top of it skin-side up, with a little space between each piece. Bake for 30 minutes, stirring occasionally, until the potatoes and carrots are fully blended. It takes 50 minutes to an hour to ensure that the chicken is thoroughly cooked and the vegetables are tender. Served with vegetables and lemon halves that have been broiled.

Braised Pork Chops with Caramelized Onion Appetizer Relish

2 people can eat this dish.

The preparation time is 35 minutes Tn!!

redients

2 people can eat this dish.

35 minutes are required for preparation. Ingredients

PORK BROTH (Brined)

12 cup papaya juice vinegar 12 cup water

2 tablespoons ali, in addition to something else to season the dish.

1 teaspoon freshly ground dark pepper (or 12 tablespoon peppercorns), in addition to something else to season the dish with

1 teaspoon of maplesyrup (optional)

2 bone-in fed pork chops (2-inch-thick)

Relish

Appetizer of medium red color

Lemon juice (about 1 teaspoon)

butter that hasn't been salted and hasn't been spoiled

Olive oil (about 1 tbsp.

medium yellow onion, diced 1 medium yellow onion, minced garlic, minced (about 2 cloves total)

Newly cleaved parsley (total of 2 tablespoons) (optional)

Directions

Place all of the ingredients in a large shallow bowl and microwave on high for 2 minutes until the water is boiling. It takes approximately 1 minute for the salt to break down. Pour in the saline solution and lower the pork to a comfortable level. Refrigerate for at least an hour and up to overnight after covering with plastic wrap or aluminum foil. Preparing the baking sheet or grill dish: Preheat the oven to its highest temperature. Shake off any excess salt water and vip it away to get rid of the slashes from the salt water. Season both sides evenly with salt and pepper, and set aside to dry out even more while you prepare the relish and other toppings for the sandwich. Chopped appetiser and lemon juice are combined in a relish bowl. Using a medium skillet, melt the margarine and oil over medium heat. Cook, stirring occasionally, until the onion is soft. It takes 7 to 10 minutes for the sugar to start caramelizing. Cook for about 30 seconds, or until the garlic is aromatic. Bring down the heat, add the appie, and mix until it is completely covered with the mixture. Dish is covered. Unti must be prepared! recentlv Actct theomon andct cook, mixing frequently,until 11 begins to caramelize, about 7 to 10 minutes total. Cook for about 30 seconds, or until the garlic is aromatic. Cook until the appie is fully cooked. Reduce the heat to low, add the appie, and mix to coat with the mixture. 1 to 2 minutes after being freshly warmed Remove the pan from the heat, stir in the parsley (if using), and set the pan aside to cool slightly. Bake for 20 minutes on a baking sheet or in an oven skillet, then remove from the oven and let cool. marginally pink in the middle, around 3 minutes for the eacb side, and still holding juices from the container 3-minute lei resi period Using two plates, divide the hacks and serve them. Pour any remaining juice from the container over the cleaves, then evenly distribute the apple-onion relish on top and serve immediately.

The following is the nutritional data: 444 calories, 28 grams of fat, 25 grams of carbohydrate, and 25 grams of protein

Taco Salad made with grilled chicken

3 people can eat this.

50 minutes are required for preparation. Ingredients: 3/4-pound skinless, boneless chicken breast halves 3 (7-inch) corn tortillas.

3cups of lettuce were smashed to bits.

2 tablespoons freshly chopped cilantro (about 1/ 4 cup)

14 tablespoons lime juice (or to taste)

Poonsstew powder (one tablespoon and one and one-half teas)

ground cumin (about 3/4 teaspoon)

ground coriander (about 3/4) teaspoon

sugar (brovm): 1 1/4 teaspoon

cayenne pepper, 1/8 teaspoon

1.5 tablespoons extra virgin olive oil (or substitute)

3/4 avocado - peeled, pitted, and cut into slices (optional)

Lime juice (about 3/4 cup) cut into wedges (optional)

Acridcream (three tablespoons) (optional)

Directions

Make a medium-high heat on an outdoor barbecue and lightly oil the grill grate before cooking.

Dark beans, salsa, 1/2 cup cilantro, and lime juice are combined in a mixing bowl and set aside.

Preheat an outdoor barbecue to medium-high heat and lightly oil the grate to prevent sticking or burning.

Blend the dark beans with the salsa, 1/2 cup cilantro, and a squeeze of lime juice in a large mixing bowl and set it aside to cool completely.

Rub mixture over cbicken breasts after it has been thoroughly mixed (stew powder, cumin, coriander, eai1hy colored sugar, cayenne pepper, and olive oil)

Preheat the barbecue to high heat and cook the chicken breasts until they are tender. 10 to 12 minutes for eacb side, as long as the middle is not pink and the juices are clear. In the middle of the sbould, there is a moment read thermometerem that reads around 165 degrees F. (74 degreesC). While the chicken is cooking, heat up some tortillas and get your grill ready to go! 3 to 5 minutes to get a nice golden brown color on the sides.

Transfer the chicken to a cutting board and cut it into long thin strips with a sharp knife. Chicken fingers should be divided among the tortillas and topped with the bean and lettuce mixture and the remaining half cup cilantro.

With avocado, lime wedges, and harsh cream on the side, this dish is a must!

Informaiton nutritionnelle There are 470 calories in this recipe, 18.7 grams of fat, 44.4 grams of carbohydrates, and 35 grams of protein.

Spiced with a touch of sweetness Chicken and Broccoli Stir-Fry Recipe

Servcs:4

30 minutes are required for preparation. Ingredients

1 tablespoon and 3/4 teaspoon low-sodium soy sauce (optional).

ground ginger (1/2 teaspoon)

1/4 teaspoon red pepper, squashed

salt (half a teaspoon)

3 34 cups broccoli florets and 2 teaspoons sesame seeds

3/4 teaspoon olive oil and 1 tablespoon sage

2.5 skinless, boneless chicken bosoms - cut into 1-inch slices (approximately).

cut green onions (about 1/3 cup)

Garlic, cut into small pieces (about 5 cloves),

Hoisin sauce (one tablespoon plus one-third teaspoon)

1/2 a teaspoon of salt and 3/4 teaspoon of chili paste

peppercorns (about 1/2 teaspoon)

Chicken stock made with 2 tablespoons and 1/2 teaspoon chicken stock

3/4 cup ano3/4 cup no1sm sauce 1 cup iau1espoon ano3/4 cup iau1espoon ano3/4 cup

1 tablespoon and 3/4 teaspoon Chile paste are sufficient.

dark pepper (1/2 teaspoon)

1/2 teaspoon chicken stock and 2 tablespoons water

Dircctions

Using a liner with no,th of an inch of bubbling water, place broccoli in a pot and cover. Cook for approximately 5 minutes, or until the vegetables are tender but firm. ***

2. In a skillet over medium heat, heat the oil and sauté the chicken, green onions, and garlic until the chicken is no longer pink and the juices run clear when squeezed.

Season with ginger, red pepper flakes, salt, and black pepper after stirring in the hoisin sauce, Chile glue, and soy sauce in a large skillet over medium-high heat. Cook for about 2 minutes after adding the chicken stock. In a separate bowl, combine the steamed broccoli and the sauce mixture until everything is well coated.

The following is the nutritional data: 292 calories, 12 grams of fat, 15 grams of carbohydrate, and 34 grams of protein

Chapter Six

Curried Beef with Winter Vegetables

Curried Beef with Winter Vegetables is a delicious dish to make.

8 people can be accommodated.

Approximately 2 hours and 5 minutes were spent preparing this dish. Ingredients

cut 2 potatoes into cubes after they've been stripped

1-cup sliced zucchini

Peel and core 2 apples and chop them up.

mince 3 garlic cloves 2 onions (peeled and diced) 3 tablespoons olive oil

Turmeric powder (1 teaspoon)

2 roasted carrots, peeled and sliced 2 roasted parsnips, peeled and sliced 2 beef ribs, chopped

or to taste, 2 tablespoons curry powder

Coriander powder (about 2 teaspoons)

Asian five-flavor powder (about 1 teaspoon)

meat toss broil with 1 inch chunks of 1/2-pound hamburger for a stew, for instance.

Olive oil (about 3 tblsp.

fresh ginger root, peeled and diced (about 3 inches long)

raisins (approximately 1 cup).

2 cashews (about a cup)

water (half a cup)

onve 011 2 (3 inch) pieces new ginger root, stripped and diced 3 tao1espoons onve 011 3 tao1espoons onve 011 2 (3 inch) pieces new ginger root

one-half cup dried cranberries

1 cup cashews (or other nut).

2/3 cup ice cubes

Recipe Directions: 1. Preheat the oven to 350 degrees Fahrenheit. 2. (175degrees C). Aluminum foil should be placed over a broiling skillet. Place the hamburger in a container with just enough water to cover it, and set aside for later. Reduce heat to low and simmer for 30 minutes after bringing to a boil. Cooking the olive oil in a large pot over medium-high heat until it is hot is the next step. Cook until the vegetables are soft, about 5 minutes, after which add the ginger, garlic, onions, and celery. Using a large mixing bowl, evenly distribute thecurry powder, coriander powder, five-flavor powder, turmeric, and salt and pepper over the onion mixture. Prepare the carrots, parsnips, potatoes, zucchini, and apples and add them at the end of the cooking process. Combine the meat, cooking liquid, raisins, and cashews in a large mixing bowl and toss to evenly distribute the seasoning. Using a slotted spoon, transfer the hamburger and vegetable mixture to the simmering skillet that has been prepared. Combine the ingredients in a mixing bowl, then sprinkle 1/2 cup water over the top. Using aluminum foil, cover the container.

Bake in a preheated broiler until done, about 1 bour, until golden.

The following is the nutritional data: 343 calories, 17.5 grams of fat, 40.7 grams of carbohydrate, and 10.3 grams of protein

Salad de Cochinita con Gingero Wraps

2 people can eat this dish.

Approximately 10 to 15 minutes for preparation. Ingredients

14 tablespoons salt 14 tablespoons freshly ground black pepper 1 pound ground chicken

No gluten soy sauce, tamari, or coconut aminos; 3 tablespoons sesame oil divided; 3 tablespoons sesame oil, divided; 3 tablespoons sesame oil, divided

1-pack green and white scallions, separated into green and white parts

minced new ginger (about 2 tablespoons)

14 teasoon red oeooerflakes, minced 2 garlic cloves, minced green and white pa1ts of scallions, separated into one pack

minced new ginger, 2 tablespoons

garlic, minced (about 2 cloves total)

red pepper flakes (1/4 teaspoon)

1. a medium-sized carrol that has been stripped and cui inlo 4-inch dice.

the equivalent of three teaspoons

Rice vinegar, coconut vinegar, and orange juice vinegar are all examples of vinegars that are commonly used.

in addition to any additional water that may be needed 1 tablespoon water

Lettuce smothered in 1 bead

Garnishing with sesame seeds

To garnish with Sriracha or another hot sauce, chop fresh cilantro (optional)

slices of lime, if you have any (optional)

Dircctions

1. Add salt and pepper to the chicken breasts and toss to coat. In a large skillet or wok, heat 1 tablespoon of the sesame oil over medium heat until shimmering. When it is done, add the chicken and cook until it is seared and cooked through, stirring as often as possible, about 3 to 4 minutes total. Transfer the cooked chicken to a bowl by using an opened spoon. lBe sure to incorporate all of the soysauce. In a small container, combine 1 tablespoon sesame oil with the scallion whites. Creating a meal requires cooking, mixing, and unti. 2 minutes is enough time for the scallions to become delicate and clear.

In a small saucepan, heat the ginger, garlic, and red pepper pieces until they are translucent, about 1 minute. Make your way to the top of the stairs.

Brussel Sprouts, Sweet Onion, and Rosemary Roasted Pork Tenderloin in a Sheet Pan

4 people can be served.

35 minutes are required for preparation. Ingredients\sPork

Pork tenderloin (about 1 pound)

Salt (about 1 teaspoon)

freshly ground dark pepper, 1 teaspoon

1-tsp. paprika, to taste (standard orsmoked, optional)

Brussels Sprouts (also known as Brussels Sprouts) are a type of sprout that grows in the Brussels area of the United States.

Managed and halved one-pound Brussels sprouts

1-inch wedges of medium yellow or sweet onion, peeled and diced

additional virgin olive oil (approximately 2 tbsp.

Mapiesynp (one teaspoon)

minced 1 tablespoon of ‘new rosemat’ (rosemary)’

Directions

425°F should be set for the broiler. Lay aluminum foil or parchment paper on a baking sheet and set aside.

Pork in focaccia is a delicious combination. when the pre-arranged baking will take place wipe it off with a sheet In a small mixing bowl, whisk together the salt, pepper, and paprika (if using). All of the ingredients should be rubbed into the meat. Mix together the Brussels sprouts and onion in a medium-sized mixing bowl along with the oil, maple syrup, and rosemary. Using a spoon, spread the mixture all over the pork. Pork and Brussels sprouts should be roasted until the pork is browned on the outside and slightly pink on the inside (the internal temperature should be 145°F). Let it rest for 3 minutes after removing it from the broiler Four individual plates should be used to divide tbe vegetables uniformly. To serve, cut the pork into 1-inch-thick pieces and arrange three or four pieces on each individual serving plate.

NutritionalInformation: Protcin 34g, 292 calories, 12 grams of fat, 15 grams of carbohydrate

A Pizzaiola-style dish of pork chops.

2 people can eat this dish.

Approximately 37 minutes are required for preparation.

A Pizzaiola-style dish of pork chops.

There are two services and the preparation time is 37 minutes total. Ingredients

1. 1 canned diced tomatoes in juice (15 oz.

herbs de provence (about a teaspoon)

134 tsp dried red pepper drops, or more to taste, if desired

1 tablespoon finely chopped fresh Italian parsley

Instructions 1. Heat the oil in a large skillet over medium heat until shimmering. Season the pork hacks with salt and pepper before grilling or roasting them. In a skillet, brown the pork cleaves on both sides until they are brown and a little crispy. After about 3 minutes on each side, a meat thermometer embedded evenly into the pork registers 160°F. Transfer the pork slashes to a plate and cover with aluminum foil to keep them warm while you prepare the rest of the meal. Sauté the onion in a similar skillet on medium heat for about 4 minutes, or until it is fresh and delicate. Combine the tomatoes and their juices, the herbes de Provence, and 1/4 teaspoon red pepper pieces in a large mixing bowl until well combined. Stew for about 1.5 minutes, stirring occasionally, until the flavors have melded and the juices have thickened a bit. Add salt and additional red pepper chips to taste after seasoning with salt. Make sure to bring back the pork hacks and any other leftovers.

transferring the juices from the plate to the skillet and turning the pork slashes to coat them with the glaze

On each plate, arrange 1 pork cleave. Toss the porkchops with the sauce until they are completely covered.

The parsley should be sprinkled on top and served immediately.

Grilled Steak that is absolutely delicious.

Serves:4

30 minutes are required for preparation. Ingredients

Cauliflower or extra-virgin olive oil (approximately two tablespoons)

boneless rib-eye or New York strip steaks, cut into 11/4- to 1 1/2-inch-thick slices

Sea salt and freshly ground pepper (kosher salt and peppercorns)

Directions

1. Take the steaks out of the refrigerator about 20 minutes before serving them.

freshly ground pepper and Kosher salt

Method 1. Remove the steaks from the fridge about 20 minutes before barbecuing and set them aside at room temperature, covered with a damp cloth.

Preparing the barbecue on high heat is essential. Season generously with salt and pepper on both sides of the steaks after they have been brnshed. Placing the steaks on the barbecue and cooking for 5 minutes or until they are a brilliant brown and slightly charred is recommended. Turn the steaks over and continue to grill for 3 to 5 minutes longer for medium-uncommon (an inner temperature of 135 degrees F), 5 to 7 minutes longer for medium (140 degrees F), or 8 to 10 minutes longer for medium-well (an inner temperature of 145 degrees F) (150 degrees F). 5 minutes before serving, transfer the steaks to a cuttingboard or platter and tent loosely with aluminum foil to keep them warm.

Seafood Recipes from Pegan (Chapter 4)

Beaches and water activities

Two srvcs are required.

Duration of preparation: 45 minutes plus 15 minutes for each additional minute of preparation.

4 ounce file of 12 medium shrimp, deveined and stripped steaks de mignon

oil (olive) (two teaspoons)

melting 1 tablespoon margarine 1 tablespoon margarine

onion, minced finely (1 tablespoon)

1-tablespoon salt and pepper for steak

onion, minced finely (1 tablespoon)

White wine (about 1 tbl)

tablespoon Worcestershire sauce (optional)

fish seasoning (about 1 tablespoon)

peppercorns that have been freshly ground

1 teaspoon freshly squeezed lime juice

dry parsley (about a teaspoonful)

Directions

1.

Pour the ingredients into a large mixing bowl and whisk until well combined. Add 1 tablespoon olive oil and whisk again. Add 1 tablespoon olive oil and whisk again.

Cover the ball evenly with your hands. 2.

Refrigerate for a few minutes to allow the flavors to meld, about 1 minute is sufficient.

A bow1, wn1sK, and 10 an a bow1 1 tablespoon each of ouve ou, omon, spreao, Worcestershire sauce,, ine, lemon juice, parsley, fish preparation, garlic, and dark pepper, all combined In a fair manner, throw tocover Allow for at least 15 minutes of chilling time after saran wrap has been placed over bowl. Preheat an open-air barbecue to medium-high heat and lightly oil the grill grate before using. 2 teaspoons olive oil should be used to coat the steaks, which should be seasoned. Unti, prepare the steaks. After 5 to 7 minutes on each side, they are beginning to firm up and have reached your desired doneness. It is recommended that you use a moment read thermometer embedded in the middle of the pie (60 degrees C). Transfer the steaks to a platter and loosely cover with a piece of aluminum foil to keep them warm. Grill until done, removing shrimp from marinade. Cook for 2 to 3 minutes per side until they are radiant pink on the outside and the meat is not straight forward in the middle.

Dietary Information: 444 calories, 34.5 grams of fat, 2.7 grams of carbohydrate, and 9 grams of protein

Chapter Seven

smoked salmon with cucumber and avocado

smoked salmon with cucumber and avocado are a delicious combination. Prepared in 15 minutes, sushi serves 2 people.
Ingredients

Nori sheets (sushi) - 2 sheets
avocado, pitted and peeled (about 1 medium-sized avocado)
Sesame seeds (isolated) 2 tablespoons (optional)
smoked salmon (4 ounces) (arouud 4slight slices)
cucumber, peeled and cut into matchsticks, 1 medium cucumber
ginger, cured in 3 tablespoons (optional)
1 teaspoon wasabi glue (or similar) (optional)
For dipping, use gluten-free soysauce, tamari, or coconut aminos.
Directions
1.

One nori sheet should be placed on a sheet of materialii paper or aluminum foil on a flat surface.

For the avocado, mash it with a fork in a small serving dish.

The nori sheet should have a 12-inch strip of avocado mixture visible along the top edge, so spread it out evenly. Sprinkle 1 tablespoon of the sesame seeds (if using) uniformly over the av. ocad.o. and mix thoroughly.

U 1v1n • •

•'>pvuuuu,..

Distribute a portion of the avocado mixture on the norisheet, leaving a 12-inch strip of nori sheet visible along the top edge. In a large mixing bowl, combine 1 tablespoon of the sesame seeds (if using) and mix well. Arrange 2 pieces of smoked salmon on top of the avocado in an even layer, covering it. Make a jigsaw puzzle out of the cucumbers. running up the length of the sheet and dividing it into sections to cover the salmon Then run the tip of your finger along the crease that has been left unfinished. When rolling away from you, use the foil as an aid, and squeeze the nori to seal it tightly and permanently. Make a second batch with the leftover nol' sbeet and fixings and place them both in the refrigerator for about 30 minutes to firm up. Make 6 to 8 pieces out of each roll by cutting it with a very sharp or serrated knife. Serve with soy sauce, salted ginger, wasabi (if using), and wasabi paste on the side.

The following is the nutritional data: 487 calories, 32 grams of fat, 26 grams of carbohydrate, and 28 grams of protein

Sautéed salmon with cream sauce

Approximately 45 minutes to prepare for 2 people

Ingrcdients

One shallot, finely minced

the almond flour (about 1 tbsp.

2 tablespoons abrasive cream

parmesan cheese (1/2 cup)

choice of 3 tablespoons finely diced shiitake mushrooms

Broccoli leaves (about 1 cup) and florets

1 tbsp capers (optional).

1 tbsp chopped chives (optional)

parsley, roughly chopped (about 2 tablespoons total)

Alaskan salmon filets (two filets)

1 tablespoon guacamole

feed butter, 3 tbspoons

minced lemon juice to taste, 2 cloves of garlic to taste, freshly ground black pepper to taste.

Directions

The fish should be descaled and washed. Fry the salmon in the avocado oil until it is golden brown. season with freshly ground black pepper to taste The fish should be scaled and washed. Using avocado oil, lightly fry the salmon for a couple of minutes, turning once (don't overcook). Using your fingers, peel away the skin and devour it! Set the fish aside after squeezing the lemon juice over it. Toss the mushrooms into a small amount of boiling water for a couple of minutes while the water heats through. Cook the broccoli florets for another 1- 2 minutes after adding the broccoli stems (should stay a smidgen cnmchy). Discard the solids after straining. The margarine should be beaten with the dark pepper, garlic and shallot in a large pot before using. Immediately after caramelization, add the sour cream and parmesan. Mix to combine, but do not overcook (about 30 seconds ablaz,ebarely long enough for the parmesan to melt).

Make small pieces of salmon and mix them into the cream.

Spiralized "zoodles" should be served alongside the mushroom-broccoli-escapades mixture. Sprinkle with chives or parsley before serving.

The following is the nutritional data: 216.9 calories, 10.9 grams of fat, 5.8 grams of carbohydrates, and 24 grams of protein.

Oil-Poached Whitefish with Lemony

Serves 4 people with gremolata

Duration of preparation: 1hr30min Ingredients

Arcticscorch or other whitefish fillets (approximately 3/4 pound each) genuine salt (one teaspoon)

freshly ground black pepper (about 1 tablespoon)

Extra-virgin olive oil (about 12 cups)

1 pound minced garlic (about 3 cloves)

14 cup freshly minced and divided parsley leaves

16 ounces ground lemon zing (from 6 small or 4 large lemons), dh ded, dh ded

Directions

Make a 13-by-9-inch baking dish and arrange the fish filets the long way in it -,.. """5 o,lVUll.l.l,UlVU """5 o,lVUll.l.l,UlVU """5 o,lVUll.l.l,UlVU """5 o,lVUll.l v IHUV V.l

Directions

Prepare a baking dish 13 by 9 inches by piacethefish filets the long way in it, seasoning with salt and pepper on both sides.

Toss together the olive oil, garlic, a generous portion of the parsley, and a generous portion of the lemon zing in a small mixing bowl until well combined. Pour evenly over the fish, cover, and marinate in the refrigerator for no less than 30 minutes and up to 24 hours before serving. 350°F should be set for the broiler. 3. Broil or bake the fish for 15 to 20 minutes, or until it is just cooked through.

Prepare the Lemouy Sautéed Chard with Red Onion and Herbs or another vegetable side dish or salad by cutting each filet into two pieces and sprinkling with the remaining parsley and lemon zest.

The following is the nutritional data: 10.9g fat, 5g carbohydrate, and 24g protcin per serving (216.9 calories).

Salad de Tona et de Mayonnaise.

Four srvcs

Ingredients: 10 minutes of preparation time

celery (half a stalk)

6 grapes (approximately),

1 container of high-quality tuna (per person)

1 tablespoon mayonnaise with a dash of cayenne

1 romaine lettuce (if available)

Drain the fish and place it in a large mixing bowl. Hands-on cutting will result in more modest pieces.

Carefully wash and cui the celery and grapes until they are perfectly shaped. Combine the ingredients in a large mixing bowl.

Use a spoon to thoroughly blend in the mayonnaise and black pepper.

Serve on romaine lettuce leaves, or cover and refrigerate for up to 1 day before serving again.

The following is the nutritional data: One hundred and seventy calories, seven grams of fat, four grams of carbohydrates, and twenty grams of protein

A Shrimp Scampi with Baby Spinach dish that is delicious and easy to make.

3 people can eat this.

Nutr1t:

Lntormat: lon AJ Lntormat: Lntormat: lon A J Lntormat: lon A J Lntormat:

It is composed of the following ingredients: (.;afo n e 170, tats 7g, carob 4g, protein 20g.)

A Shrimp Scampi with Baby Spinach dish that is delicious and easy to make.

3 people can eat this.

15 minutes are allotted for preparation.

Ingredients

Strip and devein a 1-pound giant shrimp (approximately 12).

3 tblsp. of a substance

olive oil from extra-virgin olives (divided)

garlic, minced (about 6 cloves)

chicken stock (or stock cubes) 1 cup unseasoned

Zing and juice from freshly grated ginger.

with the help of one large lemon

112 teaspoon red pepper drops, or to taste 14 teaspoon ocean sali or Himalayan sali, or to taste 12 teaspoon freshly ground dark pepper, or to taste 112 teaspoon freshly ground black pepper, or to taste

1/4 cup (12 stick) cold, unseasoned shaved grass-took care of the spread, cubed 6 to 8 cups (6 ounces) spinach leaves from a young child parsley (about 2 to 3 tablespoons) freshly chopped (optional)

In t he event that you have any questions, please contact us.

1. Using paper towels, pat the shrimp completely dry.

In a large skillet, heat 2 tablespoons of theoliveoil over medium-high heat until hot.

Cook the shrimp until they are pink, flipping once, for about 2 minutes on the evecy side, or until they are opaque. Shift onto an enormous bowlor dish. 2 Heat to medium and add 1 tablespoon oil at a time until the mixture is evenly coated. Cook for about 1 minute, or until the garlic is only fragrant. Bring the stock, lemon zest and juice, red pepper pieces, salt, and dark pepper to a boil, then reduce the heat to medium-high and simmer until the peppers have softened and the stock has thickened slightly. Reduce the sauce by half, scraping any cooked pieces from the bottom of the pan with a wooden spoon, for approximately s minutes. Remove the dish from the heat and set it aside to cool for a few minutes before serving.. Pour in the margarine in chunks, one at a time, stirring constantly with a wooden spoon until the sauce thickens slightly. Using four plates, divide the spinach evenly between them to serve. Approximately 4 shrimp should be placed on top of each plate. Distribute the sauce evenly among the plates and sprinkle with parsley on top to complete the presentation.

644 calories, 46 grams of fat, 9 grams of carbohydrates, and 53 grams of protein

11.w! - ri. 1 _....:J n - - n... - - —1 e1.... 1 _..,.. _ -.!.a.1 - n 1 t,2t,;U lJJdl t:'JlU di"VUUU 4:,unm. t"dlllll

The following is the nutritional data: 644 calories, 46 grams of fat, 9 grams of carbohydrate, and 53 grams of protein

Servcs: 2 Miso Glazed Pan-Seared Salmon with Bok Choy

Servcs: 2 Miso Glazed Pan-Seared Salmon with Bok Choy

Servcs: 2

25 minutes are required for preparation. Ingredients: 2 (6-ounce) salmon fillets 14 cup white or yellow miso 14 cup white or yellow miso

vinegar (rice or coconut): 2 tablespoons

Sesame oil, divided into two tablespoons.

1 tablespoongluten-free soy sauce, tamari, or coconut aminos, if desired

1/4 cup uew ginger, finely minced

1 clove minced garlic, 1 1/2 pounds (medium pack)

Chop the childbok choy into 112-inch pieces after removing the center and separating the white stero and verdant green parts

Scallionwhites, delicately cut into 2 tablespoons (optional)

2 tablespoons scallion greens, shaved finely, for garnishing (optional)

Preparation Instructions 1. Preheat the grill to high heat.

Place the salmon skin-side down on a baking sheet or in an oven-safe container and wipe it off. Toss the miso with the vinegar, 1 tablespoon of the sesame oil, soy sauce, ginger, and garlic in a small bowl until well combined. Set aside the remaining coating and spread 2 tablespoons of it evenly over the highest point of the salmon. If you don't have enough time, make it 10 minutes to make up for lost opportunity. The salmon should be grilled, unti. 3-5 minutes until the coating becomes effervescent Cover it loosely with aluminum foil and continue to cook until the center is just barely pink, another 3 to 4 minutes. Discard the salmon and foil from the oven and allow it to cool on a cooling rack in the refrigerator.

In a large skillet, heat 1 tablespoon sesame oil over medium-high heat while whisking the Jeft. Cook until the bok choy stems and scallion whites (if using) are tender, about 15 minutes. Remove from heat and serve! Only 2 to 3 minutes for something simple and delicate. Cook unti with the miso coating that was left over from the previous day. Cook the leftover 1 tablespoon sesame oil in a large skillet over medium heat until hot. Lastly, add in the bok choy stems and (if using) the scallion whites and cook until tender! Only 2 to 3 minutes for something simple and delicate. Cook for 30 to 60 seconds, stirring constantly, until the miso coating is fragrant. Continue steaming for as long as the bok choygreens are used up! 30 seconds after being sh1veled. Add a splash of sauce and you're done! To serve, divide the bok choy between two plates in a uniform fashion to make it look pretty. Each plate should be topped with a salmon filet and scallion greens (if using).

The following is the nutritional data: 602 calories, 36 grams of fat, 20 grams of carbohydrates, and 45 grams of protein.

Chapter Eight

Sautéed Mussels in Lemon-Garlic-Herb Sauce Broth

Four srvcs

Approximately 18 minutes are required for preparation. the edie nts of ingr edients of ingr

Mussels weighing 2 pounds

1 tablespoon extra-virgin olive oil (optional).

finely minced: 2 shallots

1 pound minced garlic (about 3 cloves)

2 cupschickenor VeggieTrimmingsStock 2 cupschickenor VeggieTrimmingsStock 2 cupschickenor

lemon juice (about a quarter cup) (from 2 lemons)

In addition to something else to garnish with, 14 cup freshly chopped new parsley diii new 14 cup cleaved (optional)

fresh newthyme (about 3 tablespoons)

14 teaspoon freshlyground dark pepper 14 teaspoon red pepper drops 112 teaspoon salt 14 teaspoon freshlyground dark pepper (optionla)

Child spinach, 3 cups (approximately) (or spinachleavesattacked more modest pieces)

1 cup cubed fresh grass (cold, unsalted)-took care of the spread

Directions\s1. In a cool running stream, rinse the mussels and, depending on the situation, remove their dark stubbles. Place the pie in a sifter and set it aside to deplete the flavor. Medium-high heat should be used to heat the oil in a large, deep skillet, stockpot, or Dutch oven. Cook the shallots, blending constantly, for about 2 minutes, or until they are delicate and clear.. Include it in your calculations.

uu.,n.l,0.,ll,1......., u v y v, 1u 11.10 vu Ul,;;ll Ul U. U V J.1, I I U.ly,, I U u..,,,

Using a buge, deep skillet, stockpot, or Dutch oven, heat the oil on a medium-high heat until shimmering. Cook for about 2 minutes, blending constantly, until the mixture is delicate and clear. Cook for 30 seconds, or until the garlic is fragrant. Blend in the stock, lemon juice, sp ices, salt, pepper, and red pepper drops (if using), until everything is well combined and smooth.. Bring the stock up to a boil, then remove it from heat. Cook, undisturbed, until the mussels open their shells, approximately 5 minutes. Remove the mussels and set aside. Reduce the temperature to a comfortable level. Any mussels that the unfortunate person has not yet opened should be disposed of immediately. Using four large serving bowls, divide the mussels evenly.

Cook until the spinach is just wilted, 1 to 2 minutes, after which remove from heat. The hotness is eliminate tbecover and a mood killer. After 1 minute, begin adding the virus spread, one piece at a time, mixing thoroughly after each addition until the virus spread is completely liquefied before adding the next. In tbedishes, ladle the stock over the mussels, garnish with additional parsley if desired, and serve immediately.

The following nutritional information is provided: 342 calories, 16 grams of fat, 17 grams of carbohydrates, and 13 grams of protein

A Salad de Crevettes et de Citrus

Serves:4

18 minutes are required for preparation.

Ingredients

an entire grapefruit or half of a pomelo

new basi sliced into 2 to 3 tablespoons

2 tablespoons of Pegan mayonnaise (or to taste)

12 bugesbrimp for 10 bugesbrimp

1/2 of a cucumber is a portion of a whole cucumber.

Lime juice or lemon juice (1-2 tablespoons) (optional)

peppercorns that have just been broken

depending on personal preference.

Directions

Pour boiling water over your shrimp and cook for a couple of minutes until they are cooked through. As soon as you're finished, put them in a colander and run a lot of cold water over them. Their shell and the tbeir vein on the back of their bodies should be removed before you begin. If you are using fresh, de-shelled, and righi now cooked shrimp, you can skip this step.

In the first instance, tho of t M 1C'nn C'11rfo,...o in the second instance, tho ofcold water logo through them,..o in the third instance,..o in the fourth instance,..o in the fifth instance,..o

The shell and vein on the back of their bodies should be removed. If you are using fresh, de-shelled, and already cooked shrirnp, do not include lhisslep in your preparations. To hold the citrus, place it on a level surface and hold it from the top. Using a large biade, cut the external piece of your citrns organic product through and through, rounding the edges (it's okay if a small amount of the organic product goes to waste when using this technique). Remove the skin from each segment by cutting it down the middle (lengthwise). Toss a major portion of mixed greens into a large bowl and top with the primary organic product (which typically has no skin). After peeling the cucumber and chopping it lengthwise, add two more limes and mix well (so you get 4 longsegments). Every one of these portions should have the biade run through it to remove a portion of the seeds (which you can eat while you're assembling the plate of mixed greens...). Using a third-inch slicer, cut the cucumber slices in thirds. In a serving of mixed greens bowl, combine the cooled sbrimp, tbc cucumber, and the cleaved basi!. A pinch of salt and some black pepper are added.

Try a small piece of the organic product from the Citrns company. If you find the natural product to be unpleasant, you are not required to add lime juice to the mixture. However, if your natural product is a little too sweet, squeeze in some lime or lemon juice (about 1 or 2 tablespoons depending on how sweet your natural product is).

the pleasantness of citrus as a primary ingredient);

Blend carefully with a spoon after you've added the mayo and mixed everything together. If necessary, increase the amount of mayonnaise used to make the sauce..

Take the righi away and have a good time with them!

With Creamy Citrus Slaw, Crab Cakes are a tasty appetizer.

2 people can eat this dish.

16 minutes are required for preparation. Lngredients are used in small amounts.

Slaw

destroyedcoleslaw mix (approximately 14 ounces)

1 medium lemon, grated zing, and lemon juice

medium navel with grated zing! orange

equal to 2 tbl Mustard from Dijon.

Grated 1 medium navel crab for Crab Cake s orange

equal to 2 tbl Mustard from Dijon.

CrabCakes

There are two gigantic eggs.

1 tbsp. Dijon mustard, grated

12 teaspoon sea salt (or equivalent)

old bay seasoning or paprika (about 12 teaspoon)

peppercorns that have been freshly ground

cooked gigantic protuberance crab meat (1 (16-ounce can), depleted and tapped dry

Cooked in the refrigerator for 34 cup

Easy Cauliflower with a fork, smash the rice

fresh parsley, sliced (about 2 tablespoons)

additional virgin olive oil (approximately two tablespoons)

Direetions

Throw the coleslaw in the blender and blend until it is smooth. In a large mixing bowl, combine the lemon zest and juice, orange zest and juice, and mustard until everything is evenly coated with the dressing. Put it in the refrigerator for about 30 minutes to set it. In a medium-sized mixing bowl, whisk together the eggs, mustard, scallions, Old Bay seasoning, and pepper until thoroughly combined. In the crab, caulilower rice, and parsley, there is overlap. Ali is gathered around the crab. Refrigerate for approximately 10 minutes, or until the mixture is somewhat firm to touch.

Removing the crab and structure combination from the cooler

divide the mixture into four patties approximately 2 inches thick and 3 crawls in diameter

Medium-high heat should be used to heat the olive oil in a large skillet or cast-iron dish. Two of the crab cakes should be added to the hot oil when it reaches a high temperature. 3 minutes per side or until the outside is a brilliant golden brown. Transfer to a plate that has been lined with a paper towel (see illustration). Attempt again with the remaining cakes. Place two crab cakes on each plate and serve with the chilled slaw on the side to complete the presentation.

The following is the nutritional data: 438 calories, 21 grams of fat, 15 grams of carbohydrate, and 52 grams of protein

Soups and Salads (Chapter Five)

Avocado, cucumber, and guava A Watermelon Salad is a refreshing summer salad.

Preparation time: 25 minutes f..,tt..,ula +C" Scrvcs: 2 Preparation time: 25 minutes f...,tt..,ula +C"

Vvaterme1on a1A - L-ucumoer avocano vvaterme1on a1A - L-ucumoer avocano vvaterme1on a1 A

2 people can eat this dish.

25 minutes are required for preparation. The following ingredients: 1 lime juice (or lemon, yet I lean toward lime)

1 cup basi that has been freshly slashed!

2 half a cup of watermelon cubes that are consistent in size

I used a mandoline to delicately cut 1 smallEngilsb cucumber.

avocado, mashed and scooped into small balls armed with a melon baller, of course.

freshly ground dark pepper and 3 tablespoons extra virgin olive oil salt to taste

Directions

1. Place the watermelon, cucumber, and avocado in a large bowl and top with the piace.

Pour the lime juice over the top and gently fold it all together. Pour in the olive oil, basi!, sali!, and pepper at the Thai point. Fill an enor mouspiale with 01110 after a delicately mixing the two ingredients.

3) To finish, 1b add a few breaks of dark pepper and torobitsofbasi! 4) to decorate with flowers

With a Garlicky Dressing, Roasted Beet and Kale Salad.

75 minutes are required for preparation. a bag of 6 red or brilliant beets (approximately 112 pounds);

Garlic (one head) 1 lb.

Divide the 12 cup plus 2 teaspoons extra-virgin olive oil into two equal portions.

1 kale bunch (approximately 1 kg) (or 6 to8 cups child kale)

vinegar or red wine vinegar (appie juice or red wine vinegar) 2 tablespoons

one-twelfth teaspoon of salt

to taste, a quarter teaspoon freshly ground dark pepper

14 cup hulled sunflower seeds, pepitas, or pistachios, toasted or raw (optional)

Directions

Heat the oven to 375 degrees Fahrenheit (gas mark 1).

Beets should be peeled and washed thoroughly before cooking. Every r should be enclosed in double quotation marks.

Preheat the oven to 375 degrees Fahrenheit.

Remove the beets and Mish from their stems entirely.

Prepare a baking sheet or broiling container by wrapping each beet in aluminum foil. To begin, remove the garlic's highest point. Place the garlic head in the foca! point of a small square of aluminum foil To make a bai!, drizzle 1 teaspoon of oil over the garlic's largest best point and wrap the garlic tightly in aluminum foil. Stack the beets on one side of the skillet and the garlic on the other. Unti, get to work. When peeled with a paring biade, the beets are delicate and should be cooked for 45 to 60 minutes. Remove the pan from the heat, open the foil pockets, and allow to cool before serving. While the beets and garlic are cooling, tear the kale leaves away from the ribs, and then tear the leaves into more modest pieces after they have finished cooling. Leaves are massaged with 1 teaspoon of oil to soften the bitterness of the leaves and remove it. Using your bands and a towel uuder cbilly running water, ship the beets to dea! " tb. Set aside the beets, which should be cut into small wedges as you go.

Ihegarlic clovesiulo a blender to make the dressing is required.

Add 12 cup oil, the vinega, the salt, and pepper after the carrots are finished steaming, and puree until it is smooth and smootb

When ready to serve, mix half of the dressing into the kale and beets before dividing it between four shallow serving bowls. " tb suuflowerseeds or goal cbeddar, if desired, should be sprinkled on top in a uniform pattern.

Season with more black pepper to taste and serve immediately.

The following is the nutritional data: Fats are 28g, carbohydrates are 51g, and protein is 11g per serving (476 calories).

a simple gazpacho made with cucumbers and tomatoes

2 people can eat this dish.

Minutes required for preparation: 5-7 Ingredients

8 plums or prize tomatoes that are particularly ripe.

Cultivated and finely chopped 1 medium red ringer pepper (about 1 cup)

1 medium cucumber, finely diced

Extra-virgin olive oil (around 12 cups)

balsamic vinegar or red wine vinegar There are 12 ne vi negar (nothing is wrong with you).

Salt

finely chopped 1 medium cucumber (about

Extra-virgin olive oil (around 12 cups)

one-fourth cup balsamieor red wine vinegar

Salt

peppercorns that have been freshly ground.

For garnish, use pepitas or sunflower seeds.

Directions

1. In a blender or food processor, combine the tomatoes, pepper, and cucumber and pulse a number of times to break up the mixture.

Once you've got the oil in, you may interact with it until it's really smooth and smootb, which should take no more than 2 minutes total. Combining both the I negar and the I negar will take a few moments.

Refrigerate the soup for about 2 hours before serving.

Salt and pepper to taste; garnish with theseed on a chilled platter.

Informaiton nutritionnelle 376 calories, 34 grams of fat, 20 grams of carbohydrates, and 15 grams of protein. 4g

Chapter Nine

Avocado with Pico de Gallo Filling

There are six steps and the preparation time is fifteen minutes.

Ingrcdients

packed with 1 1/2 to 2 tablespoons chopped cilantro

Optional: 1 tablespoon minced jalapeo

freshly squeezed lime juice (around 1 tablespoon)

Tomatoes (Roma) 2

onion, diced (about 3 tablespoons)

salt (about half a teaspoon)

3 avocados (medium to large)

Directions

1. Chop the tomatoes and onions and, if wanted, channel the liquid from the tomatoes through a fine mesh strainer.

Cut the cilantro and jalapenos into small pieces.

Diced tomatoes, diced onions, cilantro, and jalapeo peppers are combined in a large mixing dish.

Combine the lime juice and salt after sprinkling on top of the salad.

Avocados should be cut in half and the seeds should be thrown away. In order to make the hole larger, tendelry used a spoon to cut the edges of the oval orifice (which housed the seeds) (more extensive, not deeper).

Fili the avocados with pico de Gallo and serve them immediately after.

||||||||||||||||||||||||||||||||||||||||||||||||||||||||

1. ——- - - —i.- -

Avocados should be cut in half and the seeds should be thrown away. Gently cut the edges of the ovai aperture (where the seeds lived) with a spoon to increase the size of the opening (more extensive, not deeper).

The combination of fili and pico de Gallo is delicious.

Serve it as hyour favourite fundamental course, or eat it as a nibble without the assistance of anyone else.

Enjoy!

The following is the nutritional data: 174 calories, 14 grams of fat, ng grams of carbohydrates, and 12 grams of protein.

soup with coconut and lentils (curried coconut and lentils)

There are four services.

30 minutes are required for preparation. Compounds and compounds are used to make other compounds and compounds.

1 tablespoon extra-virgin olive oil (optional).

small yellow onion, chopped 1 small yellow onion, minced

minced or crushed 2 garlic cloves (optional).

1 / 4 teaspoon salt 1 / 4 teaspoon freshly ground dark pepper (optional)

12 teaspoon curry powder, or more to taste, depending on how spicy you want it.

red lentils, 12 cup (rinsed),

3 medium carrots, peeled and sliced into 1-inch chunks.

12 cups chopped cbicken or Veggie TrimmingsStock, or 1 gallon of water

Full-fat coconut milk from a can (14-ounces)

Almonds that have been chopped for decoration

Directions

Oil should be heated to a medium temperature in a large saucepan. Cook for about 2 minutes, or until the onion is tender and clear. Cook for 30 to 60 seconds, until the garlic is aromatic and the spices are well-combined.

Pour the stock and coconut milk over the lentils and carrots, and stir to incorporate. Boil for a few minutes, then reduce the heat and simmer until the carrots and lentils are tender, about

20 minutes total time. Noguarantes may be served whenever desired, or they can be pureed in a blender or food processor for a creamier texture. Mth almonds are embellished.

Amount of nutrients to consume: Nutritional information per serving: calories 372 calories 28, grams of fat 28 grams of carbohydrate 27 grams of protein

Chilled Asparagus Salad with Lemon

The letter Ty is represented by the letter I. The letter I stands for

Information about nutrition and health: 372 calories, 28 grams of fat, 27 grams of carbohydrate, and 9 grams of protein

Salad de Asparagus Chilled au Vinaigrette de Limon

Approximately 5 people may be accommodated.

10 minutes are required for preparation. Ingredients

asparagus, woody fioishes, and arugula (one package)

extra-virgin olive oil (three tablespoons)

1 lemoo of shredded ziog

Lemon juice (around 2 tablespooos)

16 ounces freshly ground dark pepper 2 tablespoons Dijon mustard 14 teaspoon salt 16 ounces freshly ground dark pepper

Red pepper chips (around a pinch) (optional)

Garnish with sunflower seeds

Prepare a large pot of salted water to the point of bubbling. Bring the dish to a boil with asparagus and unti. Aod fresh and delicate, 2 minutes of brilliant green aod.

Directly under cold running water or in an ice shower until cool, channeling and washing immediately. 30-minute cooling period in the fridge is recommended. To prepare the dressing, either wbisk the extra ingredients (except from the seeds) together until well emulsified, or shake in a tightly closed jar until thoroughly incorporated. Using two teaspoons of the dressing, divide the asparagus between two dishes and serve. Assemble a salad with seeds for crunching and/or with Quick-Pickled Red Onions if you have them on hand.

Nutritional Information: 207 calories, 22 grams of fat, 5 grams of carbohydrate, and 3 grams of protein per serving

Cocoa and ginger are two of the most popular ingredients.

Squash Soup with Pumpkin

Preparation time: 55 minutes (for 4 people). The following are the ingredients: 4 Servcs

55 minutes are required for preparation. Coconut milk (250 mL) is used as a primary component.

ncwginger, 60 grams (around 3-4 thumb measured pieces)

1 teaspoon cumin seeds (ground)

the pumpkin weighing 1 kilogram

Stock (chicken or turkey) 500 mL

coconut milk (250 mL)

ground cinnamon (1/ 2 teaspoon)

Simmering the pumpkin in 2 tablespoons of coconut oil

to taste with salt and pepper

Directions

1. Preheat the oven to 180 degrees Fahrenheit and prepare a large platter with parchment paper. 2.

Pumpkin should be peeled and sliced into even-sized slices (see recipe below).

Place the pizza on a platter, drizzle with olive oil, then toss with your hands to evenly cover the pizza.

Roast the pumpkin under the broiler for about 45 minutes, or until it is very tender and begins to caramelize around the edges..

While the pumpkin is roasting, peel the ginger and put together the remaining ingredients.

Pumpkin puree, chicken stock/broth, coconut milk, and spices

In a blender container, add the ginger, cumin, and cinnamon. It's time to mix! It's time to mix! Add salt and pepper to taste and season with olive oil.

Using a pan over the oven, heat a portion of the soup to serve (or microwave the soup assuming that is more helpful for you). Enjoy!

Informa tion on nutrition: 372 calories, 28 grams of fat, 27 grams of carbohydrate, and 9 grams of protein per serving

Broiled Broccoli with a side of salad

Serves:4

Minutes required for preparation: 5 Ingredients

Dressing

Extra-virgin olive oil (around 12 cups)

appie juice vinegar (about 2 teaspoons)

Dijon mustard (around 1 tablespoon)

I'm not sure what you're talking about, but I'm not sure what you're saying.

extra virgin olive oil (around 12 cup)

applesauce (two tablespoons)

vinegar

Dijon mustard (around 1 tablespoon)

14 teaspoon salt 14 teaspoon newyl grounddark pepper 1 teaspoon kosher salt

BroccoliSalad

4 cups broccoli florets (cut into small pieces).

12 cup red onion, thinly diced

14 cup unsalted sunflower seeds (raw or cooked)

Directions

1. Combine the dressing ingredients in a large bow and whisk until smooth.

Preparing to cover the broccoli, onion, and sunflower seeds is important!

Refrigerate for at least 60 minutes, and preferably up to a whole day or more.

The following is the nutritional data: 402 calories, 37 grams of fat, 16 grams of carbohydrate, and 7 grams of protein

Salad de Cauliflower et de Butternut Squash Rôtie

4 people may be served.

30 minutes are required for preparation.

Ingredients TheSalad

salted and peppered with 1 tablespoon olive oil

chopped 1 / 4 cup red onion

1 medium cauliflower head, sliced into florets, 1 tablespoon green onions, chopped

1 small butternut squash, peeled and cubed (about 1 cup).

Dressings are used for

half-cup vegenaise (or standard mayonnaise) 1 teaspoon chopped garlic

2 Tablespoons Dijon Mustard—It Nil Nil Nil Nil NIL NIL NIL NIL NIL NIL NIL NIL NIL NIL NIL NIL NIL NIL NIL NIL NIL NIL NIL NIL NIL

1 tablespoon minced garlic

1/2 cup vegenaise or regular mayonnaise (optional).

dijon mustard, 2 tablespoons

Season with salt and pepper to taste.

Directions

The cauliflower should be steamed first, according to package directions.

Add about 2 cups of water to a buge pot, then place a lidded container in the bottom of the container.

Bring the water to a bubbling state of affairs. Fill the inner basket halfway with cauliflower florets. Place a tight-fitting lid on the saucepan and steam for 6-8 minutes, or until the cauliflower is tender. Depending on how delicate you want your cauliflower florets to be, the cooking time may vary. Make a mental note to remove yourself from the heat and also, remove your shirt from the poi Allow for 5 minutes of cooling time after the cauliflower lochill.

Cook the butternut squash while the cauliflower florels are being steamed.

preheat the broiler to 400 degrees fahrenheit Place the butternut squash on a baking sheet lined with parchment paper or silicone baking mat, drizzle with olive oil, and season with salt and black pepper. Bake for 30 minutes. r To mix, mash the ingredients together thoroughly.

Roast for 15-20 minutes under the broiler.

Toss the cooked cauliflower, butternut squash, and red onions together in a large mixing dish.

. In a small glass bowl, add all of the dressing ingredients and whisk everything together until everything is well combined.

Pour over the salad after tasting it to make sure the seasoning is how you want it.

Everything should be combined until it is well combined, and green onions should be added to finish it.

The following is the nutritional data: 280 calories, 22 grams of fat, 13.3 grams of carbohydrates, and 4 grams of protein.

A Broccoli Salad with Red Onion and a Creamy dressing Vinaigrette made using Dijon mustard.

2 to 4 people may be served.

Minutes required for preparation: 5 Ingredients

Putting on a dress

Extra-virgin olive oil (around 12 cups)

apple juice vinegar (about 2 tbsp.

Drcssing.a..a•o•....'-A- 11,.,,J' Drcssing.a..a•o• Drcssing.a..a•o• Drcssing

extra virgin olive oil (around 12 cup)

2 tablespoons apple-juice-vinegar (or similar)

dijon mustard (around 1 tablespoon)

salt (one-quarter teaspoon)

freshly ground black pepper (around 1/4 teaspoon)

Salad de Brocoli

4 cups broccoli florets (cut into small pieces).

2 tablespoons red onion, finely diced

Sunflowerseeds, crude or roasted but not salted, 14 cup

1. In a large mixing basin, combine all of the dressing ingredients and whisk until smooth and creamy. 2.

Using your hands, gently mix in the broccoli, onion, and sunflower seeds.

Refrigerate for no less than 60 minutes, and up to 24 hours before serving.

The following is the nutritional data: 402 calories, 37 grams of fat, 16 grams of carbohydrates, and 7 grams of protein.

salad with a lot of spinach

2 to 3 people may be served.

Minutes required for preparation: 5

The following are the ingredients: 1 cup purple cabbage, shredded 12 cucumber, sliced 12 Granny Smith apple, s tripped, cored, and diced 14 cup onion, sliced 12 cup button mushrooms, sliced 1 cup cooked chicken breast, cube

nuts (cleaved) 1 tablespoon walnuts

child spinach (about 2 cups).

Dressing

12 tablespoons minced garlic, ground

onion powder (1/2 teaspoon)

Avo oil (about 3 teaspoons)

appie vinegar 1 tablespoon (about)

1 scrumptious honey breakfast

Dijon mustard scrambled in 1 tablespoon of oil.

Avo oil (about 3 teaspoons)

Appiejuice Vinegar is 1 tablespoon.

Scrambled Honey and Dijon Mustard 1 scrambled Honey and Dijon Mustard

to your liking, sea salt

peppercorns that have been freshly broken

Dircctions

In a large mixing basin, toss together all of the veggies and the cbichken.

Mix the dressing ingredients in a separate bowl until well combined. the two are well-matched

Pour the dressing over the piate of mixed greens and toss to coat the vegetables. Toss the wcll and serve the dish.

Chapter Ten

Butternut Squash Soup with Cream

8 people may be accommodated.

Duration of preparation: 1 hour 30 minutes ea. Ingrcdients

butternut squash (about 2 medium ones)

to taste with salt and pepper.

olive oil (around 2 tbsp.

1/2 cup finely chopped medium yellow onion 1/2 cup finely chopped tart green apple

veggie broth (around 3 cups)

Water (two cups)

Directions

Prepare a baking pan with aluminum foil and place it under the broiler at 425°F.

Prepare a baking sheet by cutting the squash into equal pieces and brushing the cut sides with oil and seasoning with salt and pepper to taste.

Remove from oven and set aside to cool for 45 to 55 minutes until extremely tender. Over medium-high heat, heat the oil in a Dutch oven. Using a medium-sized skillet, cook for 6 to 8 minutes until the onion is translucent. Season with salt and pepper to taste after adding the squash, vegetable stock, and water.

Bring to a boil, then reduce the heat to low and cook for 6 to 8 minutes until the onion is soft.

• Season with salt and pepper to taste after combining the squash, vegetable stock, and water.

Bring to a boil, then reduce the heat to a simmer for 12 to 15 minutes until the vegetables are tender.

With an immersion blender, puree the soup once it has cooled to a comfortable temperature.

The following is the nutritional data: 95 calories, 4 grams of fat, 13 grams of carbohydrate, and 3 grams of protein

Soup with Mushrooms in It (or Not)

Preparation time: 30 minutes ingredients: 4 to 6 people

1 tablespoonooliveoil (for a total of 1 tablespoon)

Cui mushrooms of any variety, 1 medium yellow onion, chopped Sali and pepper to taste 1 medium yellow onion, chopped

new minced garlic, 2 tablespoons

the equivalent of 1 teaspoon of newly chopped turmeric (tbyme)

Recipe: 1 cupcanned coconut milk, warmed 1 cupchicken or vegetable broth Instructions:

In a large pot, heat the oil over a medium heat until shimmering and fragrant. Season with salt and pepper to taste after incorporating the onions and mushrooms into the mix. Stir frequently for about 10 to 12 minutes, until the mushroom fluid has been absorbed. The garlic and thyme should be stirred in at this point, after which the coconut milk and chicken broth should be poured in rapidly. Prepare a stew and simmer on a low heat for 8 to 10 minutes, stirring occasionally, until the vegetables are tender. With a submersion blender, puree the soup until it is smooth and creamy, then serve it hot.

Dietary Information: 200 calories, 15 grams of fat, 7.5 grams of carbohydrate, and n grams of protein

Avocado Soup (served chilled).

4 people may be served.

30 minutes are required for preparation.

In the first half of the 19th century, the pl'honeypot was the most common type of pot. In the second half of the 19th century, the pl'honeypot was the most common type of pot.

Four srvcs

30 minutes are required for preparation. Ingredients

pitted and chopped 4 avocados (ready to eat).

3 Vegetable stock (1/2 cup)

coconut milk from a can (about 2/3 cup)

diced 3 small shallots (about 1 tablespoon each)

3 tbsp dry white wine (optional)

to taste with salt and pepper

Directions

1. In a blender, blend together the avocado, chicken stock, and coconut milk until smooth. 2.

Mix until it is smooth and well-combined.........................

Smoothly combine the shallots with the white wine as well as the seasonings (salt and pepper).

Cover and cook for approximately 6 hours after pouring the mixture into a mixing bowl.

Spoon the soup into bowls, top with diced avocado and a pinch of cayenne pepper, and serve immediately afterward.

The following is the nutritional data: A 365-calorie meal with 33 grams of fat, 14 grams of carbohydrate, and six grams of protein

Sixth Chapter: Pegan Desserts and Confections and

Choco Coconut Flour Brownies (for appetizers)

15-16 people can be served at a time

30 minutes are required for preparation. Ingredients

1 cup flaxseed meal (ground) 3 tablespoons

warm water (about 2.3 cups)

Sifted 1 1/2 cups coconut flour

Half-cup cocoa powder (unsweetened)

baking powder (1/2 teaspoon)

salt (one-quarter teaspoon)

33 cup coconut oil dissolved in warm water

Mapiesyrup, unadulterated, 1/2 cup

vanilla extract (about 1 tablespoon)

salinity (quarter teaspoon)

2/ 3 cups coconut oil that's been melted

one and a half cup pure maple syrup

Vanilla extract (one tablespoon)

Dircctions

To prepare a square glass baking dish, heat the broiler to 300°F and lightly oil it. Set aside for 5 to 10 minutes while you whisk the flaxseed and water together in a small bowl. Using a medium-sized mixing bowl, blend together the coconut flour, cocoa powder, baking powder, and salt. In a separate bowl, whisk together the coconut oil, maple syrup, and vanilla concentrate, then stir in the linseed mixture until thoroughly combined. The dry ingredients should be whisked into the wet ingredients in small clumps until smooth and well combined. Spread the bitter in a baking dish and bake for 30 to 35 minutes, or until a toothpick inserted in the center comes out cleanly. Prior to cutting the brownies into squares and serving them, allow the brownies to cool completely.

The following is the nutritional data: A 165-calorie meal with 12 grams of fat, 15 grams of carbohydrates, and 1.5 grams of protcin

Bananas with Maple Glaze

Preparation time: 25 minutes. Scrvcs: 4.

Ingredients

Peeled and cut into 5 large bananas.

3 tablespoons pure maple syrup (no additives or flavorings).

Cinnamon powder (1/2 – 1 teaspoon)

Directions

1. Preheat the oven to 350 degrees Fahrenheit and lightly oil a small glass baking pan.

The bananas should be sliced and thrown in with the maple syrup and cinnamon to make a smoothie.

Using a baking dish, spread the bananas out and bake for 15 to 18 minutes, or until they are fork-tender.

Distribute the bananas among serving bowls and top with adabof coconut cream to serve.

The following is the nutritional data: 2 g of protein per serving. 190 calories; 12 g of fat; 49 g of carbohydrates

Crunch of Blueberries and Almonds

Serves:6

The following is the nutritional data: There are 190 calories, 12 grams of fat, 49 grams of carbs, and 2 grams of protein in this recipe.

Crunch of Blueberries and Almonds

Serves:6

Ingredients: 30 minutes prep time; 30 minute prep time

approximately 5 to 6 cups of freshly picked blueberries.

1 teaspoon vanilla extract 1 tablespoon custard powder 1 teaspoon custard powder

1 cup almond flour that has been whitened

cinnamon powder (about 1 teaspoon)

A pinch of salt and pepper is all that's required.

coconut oil (one-third cup)

Almonds, quarter cup, peeled and chopped

Directions

1. The broiler should be preheated to 375° F. A pie plate made of glass is also used for this recipe.

Using a large mixing bowl, combine the blueberries, custard starch, and vanilla extract until well combined.

In a pie plate, distribute the blueberries evenly.

In a mixing bowl, combine the almond flour, cinnamon, and salt; gradually add the coconut oil, mixing well. A disintegrated mixture is formed by this process. Once all of the ingredients have been combined, spread the mixture on top of the blueberries and serve. 20 to 22 minutes at a low temperature until done. There is foaming from the blueberries, and the hull has turned brown.

The following is the nutritional data: A 275-calorie meal with 20 grams of fat, 22 grams of carbohydrates, and 5 grams of protein

Peppermint Patties that are Paleo Vegan.

It makes 24 cups of coffee. Minutes required for preparation: 5 Ingredients

one and a half cup of coconut oil

1-fluid-ounce-serving

preferred sweetener

peppermint extract 2 teaspoons 1/2 cup coconut margarine, melted

12 cup cocoa powder (or equivalent)

1-cup unsweetened condensed milk, 1 cup unsweetened condensed milk, 1 cup unsweetened condensed milk

2 tbsp. peppermint extract 1 cup cocoa powder 1/2 cup coconut margarine, melted

Dircctions

Line a 24-countscaled-down biscuit tin after the biscuit liuers and tins have been removed.

Using a microwave, melt 1 cup of your chocolate chips and evenly distribute them between the smaller-than-usual biscuit tins, making sure the sides are completely covered with chocolate.

Refrigerate.

Make your coconut margarineunti a little smoother and velvetier by liquefying it a little. Toss in your peppermint concentrate and thoroughly mix it together. Discard the firm chocolate shells and evenly distribute the coconut margarine/mini blend mixture among the remaining chocolate shells. Prepare the peppermint patties by melting the remaining half-cup of chocolate chips and strewing them on the tops of the patties. Cool until firm, then serve.

Informaiton nutritionnelle 2 g of protein, 2 g of carbohydrate, 82 calories.

Gluten-free. Chocolate Cookies that are made without the use of any flour

4 people may be served.

22 minutes are required for preparation. lngrcdicnts

chocolate chips (about 12 cup) that are extremely dull 63% of the population

Pecans, 12 cup, sliced

egg whites (about 3-4 large ones)

vanilla extract (around 1 teaspoon)

1 and a half liters

Stevia

1 cup cocoa powder (unsweetened) 6 tablespoons

salt (one-fourth teaspoon)

Directions

400 degrees Fahrenheit in the broiler

Spray with cooking spray after covering a baking sheet in baking material

Combine the stevia, cocoa, salt, chocolate chips, and walnuts in a blender until smooth.

Combine three egg whites with the vanilla and mix until the bitter is absorbed completely. Another egg white should be added if all of the dry ingredients are not completely soaked or if the mixture is too thick to pour. This dish should be extremely delicate and tacky, but not soupy.

;. ;. ;

[[

Three egg whites should be added along with the vanilla and mixed thoroughly to saturate the hitter. anotber egg wbite can be added if the dry fixings have not been soaked completely or if the mixture is too thick. This dish will be extremelydelicate/tacky, but it will be savory and not soupy at all.

Place adjusted teaspoons of batter onto a treatsheet, 2″- 3″ apart, because the treats will exte nde and spread out while they bake.

11-12 minutes in the oven should suffice for this recipe.

Allow treats to cool for 8 minutes in the refrigerator before removing them to a cooling rack.

The following is the nutritional data: Thirty calories, Tg = total grams of protein, total grams of fat, total grams of carbohydrate

Avocado Smoothie

Preparation time: 5 minutes for 2 servings Ingredients

The full-fat equivalent of 112 cup

dairy product made from coconut

12 avocados, 112 cup coconut water

spinach (14 cupcbild)

1small bunch of fresh parsley (approximately 1 pound)

1dropsteviaextract

Directions\st. In a blender, combine all of the ingredients until they're smooth. Infonnation on Dietaiy: There are 409 calories and 17 grams of carbs in this recipe. Protein: 5g, Fat: 39g

CPSIA information can be obtained
at www.ICGtesting.com
Printed in the USA
BVHW011005300622
641020BV00011B/725

9 781804 767665